craving
connection

30 CHALLENGES

for **REAL-LIFE ENGAGEMENT**

B&H
PUBLISHING GROUP
NASHVILLE, TENNESSEE

(in)courage editor

CRYSTAL STINE

978-1-4336-4567-9

Published by B&H Publishing Group
Nashville, Tennessee

Author represented by the literary agency of Alive Literary
Agency, 7680 Goddard Street, Suite 200, Colorado Springs,
Colorado, 80920, www.aliveliterary.com.

Dewey Decimal Classification: 302
Subject Heading: WOMEN \ INTERPERSONAL RELATIONS \
FRIENDSHIP

1 2 3 4 5 6 7 8 • 21 20 19 18 17

Contents

Connecting with Community More Intentionally

Introduction

The first thing you need to know about (in)courage is that you are welcome just the way you are.

It's true. At (in)courage we're celebrating seven years of sharing real life faith stories online. Well over four thousand blog posts, thousands of social media posts, dozens of book clubs, and even more small groups. Three years of coming together to share friendship stories and encouraging women to gather in homes, coffee shops, and churches for our (in)RL ("in real life") conference. Countless times hugging the necks of online friends turned real-life sisters at conferences around the country.

To say we love community might be an understatement. At (in)courage, our hearts beat for strong, healthy, God-honoring friendship. Nothing brings us more joy than watching like-hearted women connect across state lines, time zones, and languages over shared stories. Because that's ultimately who we are—storytellers who want to invite you into our living room for a cup of coffee to share what God is doing (in) our lives. There will be dishes in the sink and piles of laundry on the floor and maybe a floating dust bunny or two for you to look past. But we'll always have a seat saved for you.

And in case you were wondering if we just didn't know how to spell "encourage," we want you to know that it's only by remaining (in) Christ that we find the courage to do what the book of James calls "the hard work of getting along" (3:18 MSG). It's where we find ourselves as cheerleaders, not competitors. It's how we can encourage instead of becoming envious. And it's only through the Holy Spirit living (in) each of us that we are able to invite you into our stories—the real, the messy, the un-fine, the unfinished—but always full of hope.

Now we're bringing the online into real life with this book. Our prayer is that you would see yourself in these thirty stories, written by some of our favorite women God has brought into our lives through the Internet.

How to Use This Book

As we journey together through this devotional you'll find:

1. A short snapshot—the key Scripture, takeaway, and challenge for each chapter reading
2. A beautiful devotional to encourage and inspire
3. A list of connection questions for personal reflection
4. A connection challenge to help you move from reflection to action

We'll begin together, discovering how to connect with God more deeply because He is the ultimate example of community and friendship. As we begin to understand His promises and His love for us, we'll be better equipped to be the kind of friend He wants us to be. God loves you, friend. He wants more for you than a life of loneliness—and no matter what season you're in, whether your friendships are flourishing or He is your sole companion, you are not alone. God will not leave you, and He will not give up on you. We know it might feel like we are starting a little heavy, but it's so important to us to ground the rest of the journey here—and we hope that you'll be able to come back to this section in different seasons of your life to be encouraged.

Then we'll share stories that help us to connect with friends more purposefully—because friendship, like any relationship, takes work. And it's often the hard work of getting along that keeps us from creating deeper friendships with those God has brought into our lives—or connecting with new friends. We know it can be scary, so we'll share our failures, encouragement, and practical ideas so we can be braver, together.

Finally, we'll talk about what it might look like to connect with our communities more intentionally. It's our hope that God would give us the opportunity to love our neighbors—whether they live beside us, work in our office, care for our children, serve internationally, or deliver our mail. We'll prayerfully explore what it means to be the kind of neighbor God is calling us to be—wherever we live and whatever we do.

To relieve you of any pressure, there aren't bonus points for completing every challenge perfectly. We won't unfriend you from the community if you aren't able to complete a specific challenge in the time frame and format suggested. Our goal is that this would become a resource for you to use and be inspired by for the long term, so that when opportunities to serve or love others are discovered, you'll feel more confident to go and do what God is calling you to do.

You won't find experts on these pages, or counselors, or a self-help guru to take you on a one-size-fits-all journey to success. You'll find real women sharing real stories of what God has done, is doing, and what we hope He'll continue to do in and through our lives.

Don't worry—you'll have fun here, too! There is joy and freedom to be found on these pages and in the (in)courage community. Connecting with others lightens the load and adds space for more laughter—and healing—because we know we aren't alone. At (in)courage, you'll always find yourself among friends. Grab a cup of coffee (or tea or soda), a pair of fuzzy socks, maybe a few friends, and join us. You're welcome here, just as you are.

What comes to our minds
when we think of God
is the most important
thing about us.

– A. W. TOZER, *KNOWLEDGE*

OF THE HOLY

CONNECTING

WITH

(GOD)

MORE

DEEPLY

Starting a
New Thing

God's desire for relationship with us requires us to believe in a promise that brings change.

"Look, I am about to do something new; even now it is coming. Do you not see it? Indeed, I will make a way in the wilderness, rivers in the desert."

ISAIAH 43:19

ENGAGE

Text or e-mail a note of encouragement to a friend and let her know she's important to you.

By Crystal Stine

I t's hard to start something new. Change can rank anywhere on the scary-scale from "slightly hard" to "absolutely terrifying." And deciding to start a new thing often feels like climbing to the top of a very tall, very bouncy diving board and peeking out over the edge.

What happens if we try, and fail?

Fear holds us back from trying new things and keeps us in our comfort zones. When we're afraid to take the next step, say "yes" to where God is leading, or do something that feels uncomfortable, we find ways to convince ourselves that we don't have to do the new thing God has brought into our lives. Maybe, like me, you've said a few of these words to yourself recently:

- I'm sure someone else can do that instead of me.
- There's probably someone more qualified to do it.
- No one will notice one way or the other.
- I just don't feel like I'm ready.
- My story isn't as special as hers.
- It's been so long, I probably don't remember how to do it anyway.
- I'm sure another chance will come along later.
- I don't want to bother her with my stuff.
- My place isn't ___ enough to host a group.

Those excuses can keep us comfortable, and free us from our fear of failure, but in the process we might miss the joy that comes with trusting the new things God brings into our lives.

In high school I was asked the same question every senior has to answer: "So, what are you going to do after graduation?" While I knew the answer was "college," the details weren't completely decided. When I was deciding where to spend the next four years, I dreamed of studying abroad. I thought it would be wonderful to spend a semester in Europe, traveling and learning about literature and history, right where it all actually happened. I'd traveled to England and Scotland in tenth grade with my Humanities class and fell in love with both countries in a way that affirmed my decision to enter college as an English major (with a focus on books, not grammar).

I never did study abroad. I felt so homesick during the two short trips I did go on that I was fearful of what I would miss if I traveled for a longer period of time. Because of this, I never even applied for the abroad program.

During my first short-term mission trip to Mexico, with the Presbyterian youth group I volunteered with while I was in college, I spent a week surrounded by beautiful children and passionate high school students, but my fears kept me from being truly present. I was afraid to truly connect because I was sure I would be rejected. My thoughts were so focused on home and comfortable relationships that I missed what God was trying to have me experience in that moment.

In college I went on another short trip to Austria and Germany as part of my college's gospel choir. I boarded the plane, only to find myself calling home from France in tears. I blew through calling cards as often as we climbed church bell towers, more concerned about keeping up with everything happening at home than with embracing the experience God had planned for me.

Our hearts long for the comforts of home, but being homesick and having anxiety can keep us from making the new connections God has planned for us. This world is not our home, and we will be homesick. We will be afraid, and we will worry. We'll fear rejection, and we'll regret missed opportunities. But God never says we have to face change alone. He promises that He will be our strength (Exod. 15:2), so we don't have to rely on ourselves and our feelings to get us through.

God revealed to me recently that I have a track record of letting fear convince me that doing what I'd always done was the best choice, and in doing so, I've missed out on experiences I'll never be able to replicate. If we're being completely honest, my life is a perfect example of someone who chooses the guaranteed-to-succeed road. If it feels uncertain or I think I might end up embarrassed or rejected at the end of it, I've avoided it—regardless of how wonderful the experience might be.

I've been discovering, though, that God's desire for relationship with us requires us to believe in a promise that brings change. In Isaiah 43:19 we read that God promises He is about to do something new. In verse 18 God told His people to remember their great deliverance from the Egyptians, so why is He now telling them to forget? God doesn't want us to forget what He's done for us—but He also doesn't want us to stay in the past. *The Message* says it like this:

> "Forget about what's happened;
>   don't keep going over old history.
> Be alert, be present. I'm about to do something brand-new.
>   It's bursting out! Don't you see it?
> There it is! I'm making a road through the desert,
>   rivers in the badlands." (Isa. 43:18–19)

Isn't this good news? When you look back and remember past change and the growth that took place, aren't you thankful? God's plan and purpose bring change to our lives. We are created in God's image, and that means we reflect a God who does new things. He made the humble things holy when He sent His Son to be born in a manger. He commands us to love our enemies. Jesus spends time with and loves those the rest of the world sees as undesirable.

When we accept Christ as the Savior of our lives, we're not just saying empty words. We commit to a life of change. God makes us a brand-new thing, and He asks us to love each other in the radical, uncomfortable, change-filled way that He first loved us.

So what does that mean for the connections we're craving with God, with our friendships, and with our communities? It means we need to be alert for the new things God is doing, and ask Him to reveal where He wants us to change. It means acknowledging that change can be scary, but trusting that abiding with God and being alert to His will carries far more blessings than choosing to stay in our comfort zones. It means surrendering my desires to His desires and believing that He sees, knows, and is over every step of my journey.

HE MADE THE HUMBLE THINGS HOLY WHEN HE SENT HIS SON TO BE BORN IN A MANGER.

Maybe you feel dry and empty, having gone through a season of pouring out to others. Ask God to bring rivers to the desert places of your soul. Has your heart been in a season of wilderness and wandering lately? Ask God to clear a path in it.

Be alert, and be present.

John C. Maxwell says this about change: "Change is inevitable. Growth is optional." In our lives, we will experience change. Right now you're about five minutes older than you were when you started reading (don't worry—you don't look a second over four minutes older). Some change, like aging, is inevitable. Others—like choosing to travel abroad, write a book, reach out to a friend, start a women's ministry, host a mom's night out, or saying "yes" to the thing God is asking you to do next—require us to make a decision.

- Will we change?
- Will we do the thing fear is telling us we shouldn't do?
- And if we do it—will we grow from it?

When we go into a season of change and trying new things with an open heart, we leave room for God to grow us to be more like Him. The times that I've grown the most—as a mother, a wife, a friend, a child of God—have all happened as a result of doing something new and trusting God to equip me to do the work He's called me to do.

That doesn't mean God won't work in us and through us right where we are, without asking us to do a new thing. Some seasons in our life require us to do the hard work of waiting. Maybe in those quiet places we'll learn a new skill or discover that we're more courageous than we once believed. Or maybe God will use the talents and passions we develop to prepare us for the next door He wants to open.

Although I never left my college campus to study overseas, God used me right where I was. He wanted to create something new in my life, but in order to do that, He had to first take me through a season of removing the old, hardened pieces I'd built up like a wall. I desperately needed a river through my dry and weary soul, but before God could work on my heart, He needed to take me to a wilderness place so I could hear Him more clearly. It didn't feel like the exciting "new thing" I expected God to have for me, and while it wasn't what I wanted, it was what I needed.

In that season I had been craving connections with friends, prioritizing the thoughts and approval of others above my relationship with God. I looked to others for security and placed friends on pedestals and platforms with expectations so high they would never be able to live up to them. When it came to my faith life, I'd been doing a great job of paying attention to God on Sundays or when it looked good to the people I was around, but when it was just the two of us? He wasn't my priority connection.

So God took me on a wilderness journey that lasted for about ten years. My pride, confidence, and security in anything that wasn't based on my relationship with God were all idols—replacements for God—that needed to be removed before He could do a new thing in my life.

It was lonely in that season, and God took every bit of my "I can do this on my own and I don't need anyone" attitude and brought me to a place where all I could do was say, "God, I can't do this without you." As He began to reshape my heart, I began to see a small glimpse of His plan for my life. Not a single wilderness moment, feeling of being homesick, or failure is ever wasted—God was preparing me for what was ahead, because:

- I wouldn't crave connection if I never felt alone.
- I wouldn't know how to encourage if I never needed to be encouraged.
- I wouldn't understand how important an invitation to the table would be if I never felt excluded.

When life takes an unexpected turn and we can't see the next new thing God is planning, we can choose to grow or we can choose to retreat. God's desire is for us to be in relationship—both with Him and with others. God doesn't want to see us alone, but it takes a tremendous amount of courage to reach out after rejection, or to face your fear.

God promises to do a new thing in our lives. Our Creator God, who so uniquely formed the entire earth, knows every hair on our heads and every desire of our hearts. He will equip us with all that we need to face the changes ahead.

CONNECTION QUESTIONS

. What new things might God be doing in your life during this season?

. When it comes to change, do you tend to retreat or pursue growth?

. What kind of connection are you craving most today: God, friends, or community?

CONNECTION CHALLENGE

Have you ever had someone reach out to you unexpectedly and the timing be so significantly perfect that the credit goes only to the Lord? How did it feel to be the recipient of God's graciousness through another person? Has the Lord ever brought someone to mind for you, making it clear that He wanted you to reach out to that person? What was your response?

Spend some time thinking and praying about a friend who may need encouragement. Then, text or e-mail a note of encouragement and let her know she's important to you.

Living with Your Whole Heart

You weren't created to stand so stiff you never break— you were created for freedom.

> "I will give you a new heart and put a new spirit within you; I will remove your heart of stone and give you a heart of flesh."
>
> EZEKIEL 36:26

ENGAGE

Choose an activity that is completely out of your comfort zone, something that you've always wanted to try and decide to do it.

By Angela Nazworth

Growing up in the '80s meant some fads I'll never forget. Some fads, like acid-washed jeans, Paula Abdul, and roller rinks were more fun when mixed into one Saturday afternoon. The roller rink had everything a seventh-grade girl wanted: pop music, junk food, and cute boys. Even better, all of this was available chaperone free. My parents would drop me off at what the locals called "the Double R" with just enough cash for pizza, Sprite, and rental skates; and I'd escape into a new world of fun, friends, and freedom for three hours.

Week after week I pushed my toes into a pair of tan skates with neon-orange laces and wheels. I scanned the room to calculate my chances of getting asked to couple skate when Kenny Loggins's "Meet Me Half Way" lilted through the crackly audio system.

As often as I went to the roller rink, you'd think I might have become Nancy Kerrigan on wheels. But I never learned to roller skate. Not really. Instead of holding hands with a tall, lanky, blond boy, I hugged the carpeted wall. I kept my limbs stiff and my muscles tight as I shimmied forward. I never timed how long it actually took me to circle the rink, but I'm guessing fifteen minutes at least—maybe thirty.

One girl always passed me about seven times before I finished one snail-paced lap. I never met her, but my insides twisted up with jealousy every time she whipped past me. In addition to her effortless skating ability, she had three things I wanted: perfectly poufy bangs, a boyfriend who could couple skate backward, and her own white skates sporting sparkly purple pom-poms on the toes. I credited her speedy skating skills to the skates.

But it wasn't my rental skates that were holding me back. I wasn't brave enough to risk a fall. So I kept my gait guarded and hard. I rarely tumbled, but I never truly skated. I also never experienced all the glories 1980s roller rinks offered. I couldn't glide under the limbo stick, swish to one of the four corners, or play other games with friends. While connections sprouted and friendships grew out in the middle of the rink, I stuck with the fuzzy wall. Not living with my whole heart was, and still is, lonely.

The girl who rocked big hair and skated with ease also fell down every now and again. She and her friends often practiced tricks and techniques in the center of the rink. She didn't have a skating coach or magic wheels. She did hold herself loosely. She moved her body the way it's supposed to move in order to balance itself when wearing shoes set to motion. When she fell, she stood back up and used the knowledge she gained from the fall to try again. Falling isn't the problem. Being so afraid to fall that you make yourself hard is the problem. If I had used the skates as they were meant to be used, I would have learned how to skate and experienced the freedom to learn and grow. Instead, my stubbornness held strong to what I thought was best and resulted in more discomfort.

> FALLING ISN'T THE PROBLEM. BEING SO AFRAID TO FALL THAT YOU MAKE YOURSELF HARD IS THE PROBLEM.

What's true of our bodies also is true of our hearts. When fear, pride, shame, anger, and jealousy drive our decisions, we sacrifice fulfillment for a false sense of security that's both cheap and fleeting. Our thoughts focus on where we want to go next and how to get there pain free. Instead of connecting with our circumstances and the people present with us, we view them as competition or obstacles. The ancient Israelites knew this age-old problem well.

Many theological scholars agree that the book of Ezekiel was written over a period of more than twenty years during one of many times when the nation of Israel was a complete mess. The Israelites stopped living how they were intended to live. Instead of reaching toward the Creator and lover of its soul, Israel skirted toward a wall of false hope and derived a sense of security by clinging to imposters for fulfillment. One sin led to another, and soon they were muddled in a pit of moral depravity. A longing for comfort replaced the desire for spiritual growth, and their hearts toughened.

Gloom and doom line the pages of the first half of Ezekiel. But after the worst thing occurred—the fall of Jerusalem—the tone of the author swiftly changed from despair to hope, from chastisement to promise.

> "I will give you a new heart and put a new spirit within you; I will remove your heart of stone and give you a heart of flesh. I will place My Spirit within you and cause you to follow My statutes and carefully observe My ordinances." (Ezek. 36:26–27)

To me, this promise is God's way of saying,

Listen to me, my beloved. What you're doing isn't working for you. It can't work. You weren't created to stand so stiff you'd never break. That type of thinking only hollows your soul. It leaves you swatting at what frightens you and grasping for what appears to either fill the empty spots or numb the ache.

You were created for freedom.

You were created for freedom. Freedom to shake off the bossy voices that give you false expectations in order to belong; and freedom to scoot closer to Me—your Father who wants you to live confidently so you can fully understand that you belong and have purpose. Because you do belong. You belong in this mangled up world for this brief time in history, and you belong with Me for all eternity.

YOU DO BELONG.

Let Me help you. You don't need to move away from the wall just yet—I know you're scared. You only need to unclench your grip around your brittle, stony heart so I can free you of its burden. It only feels normal inside you because it has been there for so long. But it's holding you back. You know this is true.

I will breathe new life into that worn heart of yours. I will replace it with one that pumps purity and pushes out the poison. I will give you something new. A heart that will click and tick to the right rhythm. You can trust Me.

God's promise in Ezekiel is not intended to be an emotional lobotomy. It promises continual restoration through connection with Christ. It first comes when we accept Jesus as our Savior, but it requires relationship with the Giver of the heart for the new organ to function as designed.

During my roller skating . . . er, roller-shimmying, wall-clawing days, I experienced a brief moment where I could almost skate. I let go of the wall for two whole laps and felt ready for game time. The line for the limbo stretched thirty kids long, and I found my spot and waited. When it came my turn to roll under the stick, I stretched out my arms and moved my legs as if they were strapped to a pair of cross-country skis instead of roller skates. What happened next sent me back to the wall permanently.

The silence in the room screamed as I woodenly inched myself closer, barely bent my knees, bowed my head a smidge, and smacked dead against the limbo rod, sending it flying across in the direction of some boy trying to beat his Pac-Man record.

When I replay the event in my mind, I imagine the limbo stick colliding with the kid's Styrofoam cup of soda. However, I don't really know if it hit the boy's cup or what he was drinking for that matter. I only remember the reaction of the stunned crowd.

First there were loud gasps. So loud that I'm not even sure they fit the technical definition of a gasp. It sounded more like everyone in the room let out an airy shriek at once. Then the laughter tumbled out like a row of books falling from a high shelf, each landing with a thud against my soul. Shame stuck tight against the back of my throat as I made my way to the wall closest to the exit, removed the musty skates, hid inside a bathroom stall, and cried until closing time. I never tried to limbo again. I never left the wall again. I tried bravery and felt defeat anyway, so I decided to go back to what I knew best.

Our sin nature does a number on the redeemed heart Jesus gives us. If we stay connected to the new mercies Jesus offers every morning, our hearts beat vibrant and strong. They aren't weakened by comparison or pounded by thoughts of unworthiness. The heart that doesn't wander knows that it functions best right where it belongs. But when rebellion shoots through our marrow and old habits seduce, we find ourselves tousled, restless, and rambling in a familiar direction of simultaneous comfort and agitation. Inch by inch our hearts curdle, clot, and calcify until right and wrong align in a haze so thick we justify our meandering.

That almost sounds hopeless and it would be, if it was the end of the story, but it's not. Because with the new heart comes the Holy Spirit. If Christ abides in you, you cannot stay lost in the murky forest. Every cell that builds your existence will cry for connection with the One who exhales life. The promise of a new heart comes with the promise to rejuvenate that heart when we draw close.

CONNECTION QUESTIONS

1. Think of a time you struggled with holding tightly to something or someone. During that struggle, did you feel disconnected from God? If yes, in what ways?

2. What are the fears and insecurities that keep you from drawing closer to God?

3. Imagine placing all those struggles into a box and laying that box down at the foot of the cross—how would you feel or act differently after letting go of that weight?

CONNECTION CHALLENGE

Pray about everything that worries and excites you as you consider where in your life God might be asking you to let go of the wall. Ask Him for the courage to complete the task and for the wisdom to learn from it.

Choose an activity that is completely out of your comfort zone, something that you've always wanted to try but didn't feel brave enough. It could be as simple as spending time in the front yard instead of behind a closed backyard gate for the purpose of getting to know your neighbors.

PRAYER

Heavenly Father, take this beaten up, tired, fear-laced heart of mine and breathe new life into its veins. Draw me closer to Your desires so that they become my own. Lord, I need You. I need Your guidance, Your love, Your wisdom, Your compassion. I need to root myself in Your love so that I can return that love to others. Remind me, Father, that no human being, material gain, or worldly experience can bring me the freedom, power, and wholeheartedness that comes from fellowship with You. In Jesus' name, amen.

He Knows and He Is Near

God is near and wants to comfort, heal, strengthen, and rescue you.

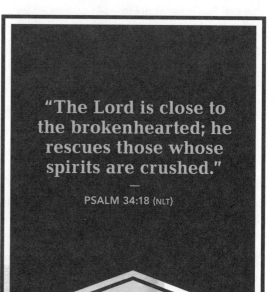

"The Lord is close to the brokenhearted; he rescues those whose spirits are crushed."

—

PSALM 34:18 (NLT)

ENGAGE

Ask God to show you who in your life could use the reminder that God is near to the brokenhearted.

W e lived in a hotel suite for three weeks while we waited to move into our new house. It sounds much more glamorous (and like the premise of a tween sitcom) than it truly was. My husband, myself, our two young children, our two big dogs, and most of our belongings were all squeezed into about 350 square feet. It was hard, and the days were long. But we tried to stay focused on the light at the end of the tunnel, which would be moving into our new house. This move and the new house were an answer to many of our prayers, after all, and living in the hotel was just temporary.

But change is hard. Waiting is hard. Cramped quarters are hard. And let's just be honest, moving is hard. Sometimes it feels like hard begets hard.

Sometimes it feels like hard begets hard.

One day in the midst of change, waiting, and non-glamorous hotel living, I loaded the kids into the car and set out in desperation to find something familiar: Starbucks. I drove around in what would be our new neighborhood, certain to find a Starbucks at any of the major intersections. Every time I would spot a Starbucks sign with the beloved green Mermaid of Coffee, it would be on the opposite side of the road or in a parking lot so poorly marked I couldn't find the entrance. It was so frustrating, and the last thing I needed in that moment was more hard. If I could just get my hands on a nonfat vanilla latte, I thought everything would be okay. I could drown my sorrows in espresso.

After too many wrong turns and no lattes, I finally pulled into a grocery store parking lot, took a deep breath, and let the tears fall. I put my face in my hands and sobbed. My kids sat in shocked silence, watching me from the back seat. Minutes passed, and the tears kept coming. "I'm okay, kids," I assured them, "everything is going to be okay." When I said it, though, it was more of a prayer than a fact.

I tried to pinpoint my problem. What was causing this breakdown? Why the tantrum? Was I really crying because I couldn't find a Starbucks? No, I realized, that would be ridiculous. I was crying because all the hard had finally piled up too heavy, and I was being crushed beneath the weight of it all. I was at the end of my own strength, and I was breaking. Just before I slipped into a self-hosted pity party, I whispered in my spirit, *"Jesus,"* and remembered that He was near.

"The Lord is close to the brokenhearted; he rescues those whose spirits are crushed" (Ps. 34:18 NLT).

The moment that realization set in, the moment my focus shifted from my crushing circumstances to my heavenly Father, was the moment my healing began. In a desperate prayer, God helped me fight off fears and lies and reminded me of His love and truth. My heart was racing and all the emotions flooded, but I knew what I had to do.

In *A Grief Observed*, C. S. Lewis writes, "The time when there is nothing at all in your soul except a cry for help may be just that time when God can't give it: you

The moment my focus shifted from my crushing circumstances to my heavenly Father, was the moment my healing began.

are like the drowning man who can't be helped because he clutches and grabs. Perhaps your own reiterated cries deafen you to the voice you hoped to hear."[1]

I had to calm my spirit down so that I could hear the Lord whisper, *"I am here."* It was as though the life raft was right in front of me the whole time, but I couldn't see it through my own splashes.

"Is anyone crying for help? GOD is listening, ready to rescue you. If your heart is broken, you'll find GOD right there; if you're kicked in the gut, he'll help you catch your breath" (Ps. 34:17–18 MSG).

I definitely felt like life had kicked me in the gut that day, and not being able to find a coffee shop was the final low blow that had me tapping out. I didn't need a latte. What I needed was peace, hope, and comfort. What I needed was Jesus. As I sat in the car and cried out to God through my tears, He helped me catch my breath. I was lonely and literally lost in this new place, but God was with me all along. Right then, as I clung to my life raft that is Jesus, I was certain of nothing else but His presence and sovereignty. His peace covered me.

Can you relate? Have you had days that left your spirit crushed? It's in those times when our spirits are crushed and we feel life's low blows that God's presence and comfort is so real it's almost tangible. When we are discouraged and our hearts are hurting, His nearness is undeniable. Just before we tap out, if we call out His name and lift our eyes, we can see hope and rescue within our reach.

We see all through Scripture how God was viewed by groups of people as well as individuals. Look at these verses:

"God is our refuge and strength, always ready to help in times of trouble" (Ps. 46:1 NLT).

"My God is my rock, in whom I find protection. He is my shield, the power that saves me, and my place of safety. He is my refuge, my savior, the one who saves me . . ." (2 Sam. 22:3 NLT).

What comes to mind when you hear the word "refuge"? I picture a big, strong umbrella, a barricaded safe place, or sometimes a lighthouse. It's a place that is warm and protected from elements and enemies, and when I'm in a refuge, I'm completely safe. This is what the Lord is to His children. A Rescuer drawing us into His refuge.

Hold these truths close and cling to them. See Him as your rock, your refuge, and Savior.

What if I had found a convenient Starbucks that day? What if I had never had to pull over and cry it out? Would I still have this understanding of God's presence? Would I know the realness of Psalm 34:18? I wonder if I was on a divine route that day that led me to a parking lot where I would learn firsthand that God is near to the brokenhearted. Maybe I wasn't lost after all.

GOD IS NEAR TO
THE BROKENHEARTED.

Being part of a Bible teaching church, attending Bible studies, and surrounding myself with friends who speak truth have allowed me to have Psalm 34:18 and other Scriptures in my internal heart-shaped Rolodex. I had heard and read that Psalm before, but never had I needed to claim it for myself more than I did that day. Staying connected to God's Word—regularly reading it, writing it, praying it, and studying it—helps me to know His promises when I need them the most. All these mornings when I wake up, go to my corner on the couch, open my Bible and read, God's promises are being planted in my heart. And every day that I tend to the soil in my spirit, His promises take root. And when I am struggling or hurting, the harvest is being able to recall God's truth for comfort, peace, strength, and hope.

His Word is what held me together when it felt like all else was falling apart. In that season when everything seemed unstable, unknown, and hard, His promises were sure. My spirit was crushed, but I found hope when I sought the Lord.

He's there for you, too, friend. In every hurt, every hard day, every disappointment, and every heartbreak God is near and He wants to comfort, heal, strengthen, and rescue you. When you are lonely or lost, whether literally or figuratively, the Lord holds out His hand to reassure you of His presence. He is hope. He is always there to rescue those whose spirits are crushed. Stop splashing and reach for the life raft. Call out His name.

HE IS ALWAYS THERE TO RESCUE THOSE WHOSE SPIRITS ARE CRUSHED. STOP SPLASHING AND REACH FOR THE LIFE RAFT.

He is near, and He knows. Are you hurting today? Is the hard piling up and weighing you down? Is your spirit starting to feel crushed? Cry out to Jesus, friend. God is listening and ready to rescue you.

I found something remarkably more than a Starbucks that day: I found my peace in the Lord. And as my family settled into that season of change, I was able to rest in knowing He is near despite the hard.

We've lived here for three years now, and I can tell you exactly how to get to the three nearest Starbucks locations, which side of the road they are on, and even which one has the best baristas. More important, I can recall Psalm 34:18 any time I need that comfort and reassurance. It's amazing how one small sentence from my Bible— one nugget of truth from the Word of God—can soothe my weary soul. Hard begets hard, yes, but our God is able. I hold it close to my heart knowing that the Lord knows and He is near.

Hard begets hard, yes, but our God is able.

Let Him minister to your life and lift you up once more. Let Him heal your broken heart, lift up your crushed spirit. Let Him bring restoration as you lean on Him.

CONNECTION QUESTIONS

1. What truth from Scripture brings you hope when your heart is broken?

2. What is your "latte"—your false sense of comfort?

3. How does understanding Psalm 34:18 impact the way you connect with friends and with your community in hard and challenging times?

CONNECTION CHALLENGE

In times of discouragement and when hard begets hard, isn't it nice to be reminded of God's presence and promises? When we can relate to the heartbreak and to the rescue, we can offer hope to someone else who might feel crushed beneath the weight of life today.

Look for two or three Scriptures or song lyrics to remind yourself that God rescues those whose spirits are crushed. Keep them where you can easily see them and look for moments to share them with a friend who might need an encouraging word.

PRAYER

Father, thank You for the promises of Your Word. Thank You for being close to the brokenhearted. Lord, thank You for rescuing us when we are crushed. Thank You, Father, for being our source for comfort, hope, and peace. Heavenly Father, draw us nearer to you when we feel lost and alone. Strengthen and cover us, God; bring a reminder and understanding that You alone are the ultimate need in our lives. Lord, thank You for Your faithful promises and Your unfailing Word!

Random Acts of Hope

CONSIDER

Our hope is grounded in our relationship with Jesus Christ.

"This hope will not disappoint us, because God's love has been poured out in our hearts through the Holy Spirit who was given to us."

ROMANS 5:5

ENGAGE

Plan a random act of kindness—or hope—today, even if it makes your heart hammer and your palms sweat.

By Anna Rendell

It was Christmas Eve day, and I was running errands in our old minivan with the squeaky brakes and worn upholstery, my four-year-old strapped into his car seat in the back. We pulled into a coffee shop drive-through, and my heart started thumping.

Before we even left the house I'd prepped my son for our mission. "It's Christmas," I said, "and today we're going to spread some joy." We'd made an adventure of being in good spirits, and now were going to wrap up our outing by paying for the order of the vehicle behind us in the drive-through.

Anonymous random acts of kindness work well for my introverted heart, but I still get nervous about drawing attention to myself.

I ordered for us—mine a big peppermint mocha because "'twas the season," his an itty bitty caramel apple cider—and squeaky braked our way to the payment window. My throat was getting dry as I leaned out my window to tell the barista that we'd be picking up our neighbor's tab as well.

She met me halfway out her window and said that the car ahead of us has covered a portion of our bill. I stammered something about how that was what I was going to do, too, and her sunbeam smile said Merry Christmas.

But then she said that our order wouldn't be ready for a moment yet—could we pull around the corner and they'd bring it out?

My attention-avoiding heart began hammering again. That meant our cover would be blown. As the car behind us drove by me, they'd look at me. And what if they were offended or thought I was showing off or seeking attention? What if they rejected my offer of kindness? My son was crowing in the backseat, thrilled with our small good deed, while his mama was sinking into the foam poking through the worn seat cover, terrified of being seen.

We pulled over to wait for our drinks, and eventually the car we'd paid for pulled around. I cringed, waiting for the scene I knew would come.

And of course, it didn't.

Their car slowed as they passed us, honking and waving, beaming out the window. They were nothing but delighted, and I was too. We'd loved others from the Spirit inside us, not from our own flesh, and He had been gracious despite our fear.

What is this fear that creeps into kindness, into hope, and why do I allow it to take center stage? I recall moments in friendships when a risk had to be taken—a move made so we could continue forward—and my heart would panic, stomach in my throat, mind made up that the ending would be painful.

Yet when these friendships—when our hearts—have even a bit of Christ in them, hope does not disappoint, because He promises to be faithful. God promises to be our friend and the basis of our friendships. He promises, and He delivers.

My pessimistic heart has a tendency to scoff at hope. "Prepare for the worst," it whispers. "Don't dare believe it could end well—that way you'll be ready if it doesn't," it beckons. "Protect yourself. Keep your distance so you don't get hurt," it smirks. "Being her friend won't be worth the risk," it lies.

Hope feels dangerous to me.

Hearts could break if we dare hope. Rooms could close in, cheeks could flush scarlet, and situations could get all kinds of awkward if we dare hope. Dreams could be crushed if we dare hope.

Yet Scripture tells us that hope won't disappoint us after all. In fact, we rejoice not only in the glory of God, but also in our affliction that:

- produces endurance
- produces proven character
- produces hope (Rom. 5:2b–4, author's paraphrase)

Our hope is grounded in our relationship with Jesus Christ, which is guaranteed not to disappoint.

I was six years old and wearing black patent leather shoes when hope in friendship failed me for the first time. The pastor had told us that it was good to be friends. Friends are fun, friends are nice, and friends are what we're supposed to be. He told us to ask someone new to be our friend, and wouldn't it be nice when they said yes?

But the girl I asked said no, she didn't care to be my friend.

She laughed a little, and I walked away feeling foolish and deeply hurt with my head hanging low. I still remember what the tiles of that church basement looked like, and I've never forgotten how it felt to be denied friendship.

At six years old, it stung.

At sixteen, it broke my spirit.

At twenty-two, it corroded my heart.

And at thirty-four, it brings a dull ache.

To not be invited, to have kindness rejected, can dash all hope.

Book clubs meet, coffees are sipped, stores are shopped, play dates had, and someone is inevitably left out. As an adult, I anticipated friendships would become easier for me, but I've found that they can be even more difficult. There are more schedules to juggle, feelings and fears are more deep rooted, intentions more difficult to interpret, and comparisons are easier to make. And the last thing we want is for someone else to feel these same things from us.

Yet often the longing for friendship is the same as when we were younger. Even though the activities of friendship may change (although painting our nails and having sleepovers never gets old!), the underlying heart desires remain. When it comes to friendships and being in community, our heart of hearts is the same. We want to:

- Be invited.
- Sit together for a meal.
- Share our hearts and be understood.
- Stay up late talking and laughing.
- Do fun things together.
- Cry together.
- Hug each other.
- Have a conversation using only a look.
- Be known.

Friends refill us. Friends refresh us. Friends refuel our souls . . . but only if we let them.

Friends refresh us. Friends refuel our souls . . . but only if we let them.

And it can be hard to let them, because the hurt we may experience only grows with our hearts and age. Now we know the risks. Now we know what we're missing out on. Now we know that to be denied friendship can feel like a reflection of who we are . . . but sister, it isn't.

It isn't foolish to reach out, hoping to build a friendship. It isn't foolish to take the first step, trying to further a friendship. It isn't foolish to extend a hand, desiring to repair a friendship.

Having and holding hope isn't foolish, but it is risky.

She could say no. She could laugh at you. She could hurt you. Sure, she could—but even if she does, God won't allow it to go to waste. He's in the business of redemption, and ultimately our hope is in Him.

Friends, Christ *will* make all things new, and He *will* recycle our pain for good. I've experienced this in my life and seen it over and over again in the lives of those around me.

CHRIST WILL MAKE ALL THINGS NEW, AND HE WILL RECYCLE OUR PAIN FOR GOOD.

In high school I had a big fight with a friend resulting in an abrupt ending to our friendship. We never spoke after that. For years I lived with regret but made no moves to ask forgiveness, even though I did run into her from time to time. Not long ago I was walking into a store as she was walking out. We made small talk there on the cold sidewalk for a few minutes, but instead of using the opportunity to make amends, I chickened out AGAIN. I said good-bye with a sinking heart and a wallowing spirit.

Not a very heartwarming story of friendship, but I learned three things that day:

1. Always take the risk. I was so scared that she would reject my apology I simply didn't make one. Now, years later, I wish I had apologized for my part in our split when I had the chance. While I'm still working on bravery in friendships, I'm much more likely to take risks with my friends because of the one risk I didn't take.

2. Humility can lead to freedom. If I'd swallowed a piece of humble pie and asked forgiveness, my heart may have been lighter. Instead, I've asked God to help me let it go and to be brave if I ever have the chance to see my friend again. There's a lightness in spirit that comes with forgiving and being forgiven. I'm quicker to apologize now and hope that my friends can do the same with me.

3. Remain hopeful. I have hope that I will run into my old friend one more time, and my first words to her will be, "I'm sorry." Losing the chance to right a wrong

actually makes me hopeful for just one more encounter with her.

God recycled that painful exchange into a new depth of friendship with others. He took the lessons I learned and channeled that learning into other friendships. He made beauty from ashes, and I am a better friend and a better woman because of His faithfulness. I've taken risks with other women, I've pursued friendships in hope rather than shrinking from them in fear, and I haven't let another walk away without resolving the hard thing between us.

Have you ever been afraid of friendship? When I'm scared of friendship, I have to step back and evaluate: Why am I afraid? What exactly do I think will happen if I fully engage, ask that big question, encourage without reservation? What happens if I offer love? Why do I fear being disappointed?

Pain is inevitable. We will hurt one another. In the last year alone, I've experienced pain in friendships dissolving, my friends being hurt, lies spoken, changes in friendships, guilt from limited time to engage, faraway friends who needed a hug, jealousy (both ways), unmet expectations (both ways), and rejection. And that's coming from a friendship-wary introvert! Each one by itself is hard, but combined they are enough to hang up my hat on friendship forever.

But then I look at my kids, and I remember watching my mother model life-giving friendship to me as a child.

My mom was a single parent. While working full-time as a teacher and working part-time at our church, she parented my two siblings and me and did not have time for the "luxury" of friendships. However, even though I never saw her leave for a girls' night out or coffee with a friend, I did see her talk on the phone. The long, blue, spiral cord of our kitchen telephone wrapped around the island and into the living room, allowing my mom to talk to her friends while we were doing homework or getting ready for bed. She talked to them almost every night, a small circle of women I still respect and love. Though not often, the few times they did get together was a whole family affair (not very calm for the mamas). These women did friendship in the way that worked for them, and it was worth it.

In her quiet, under-the-radar way, I saw my mom fight for friendship in a season that was completely consuming and full, no white space in the squares of our family calendar. She held on to hope despite hurt and restricted time.

May my children also see their mom fighting for friendship.

May they see their mom making connections, dropping by, dragging the (now non-existent) telephone cord around the house as I talk to my friends. May they see their mom forging ahead in hope, doing friendship in her own quiet way, modeling love and being intentional with friendships. Even though I've walked through pain in relationships, I've also held onto hope and been brought to tears by the beauty experienced in them.

Friendships are a gift. In just the last year, my friends have rallied around our family in prayer, brought meals on cold nights, prayed earnestly for me, cared for my kids, laughed and cried with me, taken chances on me, sent text messages to check on me, worshipped alongside me, spoken truth into my heart, invited me, driven miles to see me, answered their phones, sent cards, and made gifts. They have loved me well. My friends have refilled me, refreshed me, and refueled my soul because I've let them in, knowing that having hope in God's design for me to be in community will not disappoint my heart.

Friendship—and the work it takes—is worth the risk, and so is God's love. The chances we take on friendships are never wasted.

Even if the friendship doesn't deepen, our relationship with Him will. When we draw closer to others out of the overflow of His love in our hearts, we draw closer to Him. What we learn from our friendships can apply to our friendship with God, and what He teaches us of friendship can only strengthen ours. But we have to first choose to take the risk.

Friendship—and the work it takes—is worth the risk and so is God's love.

And in Christ, all we have to lose is ourselves.

We only find ourselves—and our true friends—once we've laid them down. He is good, and His friendship won't disappoint us. We are able to hope abundantly in Him for our friendships because He has already poured His Spirit into our hearts, and that Spirit and His love will never disappoint.

CONNECTION QUESTIONS

1. Think about one painful experience in your life that God recycled for good. What fruit came from it? How did He prove faithful?

2. God promises a hope that will not disappoint. But have you ever felt that hope *did* disappoint you? How did God bring redemption from that place of disappointment?

3. Consider a friendship in your life that you value. What hopes do you have for it? What risks could you take that could help grow the friendship?

CONNECTION CHALLENGE

God's kindness to us through Christ should be the motivation by which we bless others and help them to see the hope we experience daily because of Christ. Christ is our example. He showed us how to love, serve, and bless people around us. God will never waste an act of kindness—or one of hope!

Plan a random act of kindness—or hope—today, even if it makes your heart hammer and your palms sweat, and trust that God will work in and through you.

How Are You, Really?

There's nothing that can hinder community and friendships more than us not needing each other.

"But he said to me, 'My grace is sufficient for you, for my power is made perfect in weakness.' Therefore I will boast all the more gladly about my weaknesses, so that Christ's power may rest on me."

—

2 CORINTHIANS 12:9 (NIV)

ENGAGE

Ask a friend how you can pray for her—no "fine" allowed!

By Renee Swope

Should I be honest?" I wondered. "What if I start crying? What if she doesn't really have time to listen? What if she is just asking to be nice? I could keep it simple and tell her I'm fine."

There I was, standing in the lobby at church waiting for my husband to return from the children's ministry area, when an old friend walked up and asked how I was doing. Our three-year-old daughter had been diagnosed with a severe speech disorder a few weeks earlier, and I was not "fine."

I was exhausted. I was overwhelmed. And I was afraid my little girl might never be able to talk.

Yet I felt like I shouldn't be any of these things. I should have more faith, more stamina, more strength and courage to navigate the unknown path of special needs parenting.

Sometimes it's hard to let people know how we're *really* doing because we don't want to be high maintenance, right? We don't want anyone to feel sorry for us. Or we fear if we're honest, someone might perceive our struggle as a lack of faith.

The one thing a hurting heart doesn't need is a "sidewalk sermon" that translates into guilt because we perceive others expect us to be stronger. We've all had a well-intended Bible verse poured over our problems like peroxide, hoping it will wash all our un-fine feelings away. But when our hearts need more than a Scripture promise, we feel like failures.

Sometimes the risk of being misunderstood or judged feels so great, we think we have to pretend we're fine.

Sometimes it's hard to let people know how we're really doing because we think they are only asking to be nice. It's easy to believe they don't really care to know, don't have time to listen. What if we're honest and it gets awkward because they don't know what to say?

Yet there are those times when someone sincerely wants to know and we just don't want to tell them. That is the place where things get tricky for me.

I will tell people I'm fine even when I'm not, because I want to be. I don't want the struggle that's in front of me. I don't want to be weak and broken. I want to be okay. I want to feel strong, resilient, and courageous.

Or, I will tell people I'm fine because I hope that by saying, "I'm fine" eventually I will be. Like somehow verbalizing what I want to feel could be a predicting factor in how I might turn out one day.

Other times I think we're afraid to be honest because if we tell someone we are feeling insecure or inadequate, they might start seeing us as someone who IS insecure, weak, and inadequate. When really, the struggle was temporary. Not a permanent lens through which to view us.

And then there are times I act like and tell others I'm fine because I think that's what people expect of me.

Of course there are days when my hormones trump all good manners and, if my people are within ten feet, they know I am NOT fine. In fact, if I tell them I am, what I really mean is that I am:

Frazzled,
Irritated
Neurotic, and
Exhausted!

But not in public. Not where I try to keep people from seeing the "F.I.N.E." deep inside me.

And that is where I stood that day in the lobby at church. At a pivotal point of decision. Should I be honest and let my friend see the real me? Should I tell her how I'm really doing?

Everything in me wanted to keep my guard up, keep my heart sealed off and my lips sealed tight.

But I was tired. Tired of pretending I was fine.

So I took a risk. I let my heart, my words, and my tears spill. I shared the hard parts of countless assessments and an unexpected diagnosis, and the heartache of not knowing if our little girl would be able to talk for years.

Kelly listened. Although I know she probably had places to go, she stayed with me. She grabbed some tissue when the tears started down my cheeks. And she asked if there was anything she could do to help.

When I wanted to be strong, God showed me the powerful gift of being weak.

> WHEN I WANTED TO BE STRONG,
> GOD SHOWED ME THE POWERFUL
> GIFT OF BEING WEAK.

Paul describes what happens when God allows struggles that make us feel weak. And what God does in our weakness when we're willing to rely on Christ. God's power comes and rests on us.

> Therefore, in order to keep me from becoming conceited, I was given a thorn in my flesh, a messenger of Satan, to torment me. Three times I pleaded with the Lord to take it away from me. But he said to me, "My grace is sufficient for you, for my power is made perfect in weakness." Therefore I will boast all the more gladly about my weaknesses, so that Christ's power may rest on me. (2 Cor. 12:7b–9 NIV)

Right before this passage, Paul had described incredible visions and revelations God had given him, but then he switched gears in his letter to his friends in Corinth. There was a clear shift from focusing on his weakness to boasting in the Lord's faithfulness.

God allowed Paul to struggle with a weakness he had asked God to take away. But God allowed this hardship to continue, and in this passage of Scripture Paul

explains how God was protecting him from pride and the danger of becoming self-sufficient.

There's nothing that can hinder community and friendships more than us not needing each other. Like Paul, I think God wants us to become more comfortable with our weaknesses because it keeps us dependent on Him and needing each other.

Our weaknesses are the things that keep us connected because they are what we have in common. They are the pathways to intimacy because we can encourage one another when we meet someone going through a trial like the one we just survived. Or vice versa.

And we all have them: trials, struggles, and weaknesses just like the apostle Paul describes. As John Piper explains, "What Paul summarizes as weaknesses in verse 9, he spells out in four other words in verse 10: insults, hardships, persecutions, and calamities.

- Insults—when people think of clever ways of making your faith or your lifestyle or your words look stupid or weird or inconsistent.
- Hardships—circumstances forced upon you, reversals of fortune against your will. This could refer to any situation where you feel trapped. You didn't plan it or think it would be this way. But there you are, and it's hard.
- Persecutions—wounds or abuses or painful circumstances or acts of prejudice or exploitation from people because of your Christian faith or your Christian moral commitments. It's when you are not treated fairly. You get a raw deal.
- Calamities (or distresses or difficulties or troubles)—the idea is one of pressure or

crushing or being weighed down; circumstances that tend to overcome you with stress and tension."[2]

Circumstances and situations and experiences and wounds that make us look weak are things we would probably get rid of if we had the human strength.

- If we were "strong," we might return an insult with such an effective put down that the opponent would wither and everyone would admire our wit and cleverness.
- If we were "strong," we might take charge of our own fortune and turn back the emerging hardship and change circumstances so that they go the way we want them to and not force us into discomfort.
- If we were "strong," we might turn back the persecution so quickly and so decisively that no one would mess with us again.
- If we were "strong," we might use our resources to get out of the calamity or distress as fast as possible, or take charge of the situation and marshal our own resources so masterfully as to minimize its pressure.

But we are not always going to be strong, and that is a good thing. "That is why, for Christ's sake, [we can] delight in weaknesses, in insults, in hardships, in persecutions, in difficulties. For when [we are] weak, then [we are] strong" (2 Cor. 12:10 NIV, author's translation in brackets).

We don't need to keep pretending we're fine. What we need is to have (and to be) a friend who will say, "You don't have to be strong all the time." A friend who will give us permission to be weak and remind us of the truth we so easily forget: God's power shows up in our weakness when we're willing to be real about our struggles and our need for His strength.

What I needed and what God provided that day in the lobby of my church was a friend who listened with compassion and concern and prayed for me.

Before we went our separate ways Kelly asked if she could pray for me, right there in that moment. Afterward she thanked me for being willing to be honest and tell her what was *really* going on. She told me how often she looked at my life and assumed I was fine and had it all put together.

But that day, knowing I needed help, prayers, and encouragement—and didn't have it all figured out—she felt more "normal."

God is able to work His grace and His strength in our weakness. When we're willing to be weak, He gets to be strong for us. When we're willing to be real, others get to see, pray for, and know the "real you" and the real God we so desperately need and love.

CONNECTION QUESTIONS

1. When someone asks how you are doing, or how they can pray for you, is it hard to be real with them about struggles you're facing? Are you tempted to say you're fine when you're not really doing that great?

2. In your moments of struggle, frustration, or panic, are you able to be honest and vulnerable with God, or do you feel like you need to be "fine" with Him, too?

3. How can you be un-fine with someone today?

Lord, it's so easy to feel like I should be strong when I'm not. The truth is, I'm weak but I don't like to show it. It's hard to be real with other people, and sometimes it's hard for me to be real with You because I think You expect me to have more faith and courage. Help me remember that in my weakness, I can depend on You and Your strength. I want to be so secure in You that, like the apostle Paul, I'm not afraid to admit my weaknesses because I know that's where Your power shows up and Your glory shows off when people see my need for You.

CONNECTION CHALLENGE

It might feel uncomfortable at first, but let's practice being un-fine with one another. Before you connect with a friend, decide that you will go first and be brave by being vulnerable about something you're walking through that is making you feel weak or inadequate and in need of God's strength.

Ask a friend how you can pray for her. Maybe send her a text or give her a call and invite her to lunch so you can see each other face-to-face. Take time to catch up and ask how she is REALLY doing—no "fine" allowed!

When You Feel As If There Must Be Something More

CONSIDER

Our hearts crave connection that God longs to fill.

"Wait for the Lord; be strong, and let your heart take courage; wait for the Lord!"

—

PSALM 27:14 (ESV)

ENGAGE

Ask God to open your eyes to His plan for the day—as you seek His agenda over your own.

By Deidra Riggs

Even now, my husband and I sometimes talk about conversations we had early in our marriage when I would throw out the question, "Who will be my friend?" This question proved to be more complex than it may seem at first glance, and it took years to see how it would be the tool God used to keep my attention.

Harry and I married young. I was twenty-two, he was twenty-four. By the time I was twenty-seven, we had two children and my husband was a few years into his very first pastorate. We lived in a small, Southern, rural community where most of the church members were related to each other. Sweet tea was the drink of choice, weekend afternoons in a rocking chair on the front porch served as recreation, and the barber shop across the road from the church was the hub for catching up on the latest news or finding out where to buy a roast for Sunday dinner.

When my husband received the invitation to move south from our hometown in Michigan, I had just given birth to our firstborn son, Jordan. I was holding that small baby in my hospital bed when Harry walked in one morning to tell me the church had extended an offer. Within ten weeks we reached a favorable agreement with our landlord, and we had Jordan dedicated in the front of the congregation at our home church. A crew from the new church drove up to Michigan, packed up a U-Haul, and took our furniture ahead of us. Then we drove for two days until we arrived in the driveway of this new (to us) church's parsonage.

I arrived there, sight unseen.

I'd been too pregnant to make the trips with Harry when he was interviewing for the job. He had done his best to describe the community, the church, the congregation, and the little white house we'd be calling home. The last two hours of our drive from Michigan to this gravel driveway had taken us, in the dark, around hairpin curves, up steep climbs, and then through deep descents. After successfully keeping my most recent meal from making an appearance,

I now stood in the family room of the parsonage with Jordan asleep in my arms. My knees were weak, my head ached a bit, and my stomach was tender with both travel sickness *and* homesickness.

I took in the mauve carpet and the mauve walls. I looked at our mismatched gaggle of hand-me-down furniture, piled up in front of the door so high there was barely enough space for Harry and me to stand in the entrance without a chair leg digging into our ribs. I don't know what I had imagined, but this new home at the foothills of the mountains was not it, that's for sure. "Well," I said to Harry, "*you* can stay here, but me and this baby are not." It wasn't home, and it wasn't homey. At least, not yet.

All my friends and family were hundreds and hundreds of miles away. My stomach hadn't quite recovered from our adventurous romp over the mountain, and I was working hard to fight back the tears welling up in my eyes and the lump rising up in my throat.

But my husband is not one to back down from a challenge. In addition to that, he loves his family deeply. I'm sure he must have panicked when he heard me say I wouldn't be staying in that house that night. I mean, where was I going to go? We definitely didn't have money for a hotel. And, like it or not, this place where we were standing was, indeed, our home. I didn't really have a choice. So, right then and there, Harry started clearing that furniture away from the door. We found the crib, the mattress, some sheets and a blanket and laid Jordan there to finish sleeping. And slowly, the parsonage began to look like I could sleep there after all.

While Harry kept clearing a path through our stuff, I found our bed in the back bedroom. We worked late into the night. I set up our tiny bedroom, making up the bed with our sheets and comforter. The familiar fabrics and patterns helped to settle my stomach and my soul. These items felt like home. Harry made his way, back and forth from the house, out into the darkness, bringing our few additional possessions from the car into the house. Somehow, it all began to come together and, while I was still a very long way from my family and friends, my church community, and my favorite grocery store, I still had my son, sleeping peacefully in his small bedroom, and my husband, standing faithfully by my side.

We did sleep in that house that night. All three of us. And we kept sleeping in that house. Harry served that church, and the members of the congregation loved us well. They became like family to us, and the parsonage became home. We painted. We had repairs done to the house. We made friends. We endured sickness and loss. We celebrated birthdays and anniversaries. We fell in love with the mountains and the blue skies and clothes drying on the line in the backyard. We planted a garden. We got pregnant again, a girl this time. When she was born, we named her Alexandra. Life was good.

Don't hear me say things were perfect. There were times that were tough, like walking into that parsonage on the very first night, or navigating life with small children while living so far away from my parents and Harry's parents. Overall, however, our life together was beautiful. But deep in my soul, in some persistent part of me, I kept feeling as if I needed more.

The very first time I asked the question, Harry and I were in our bedroom. He was getting ready for the day, and I was sitting on the bed, looking out into the distance. "What's up?" he said to me, clearly sensing something was on my mind. Not having formulated the question in my head, I was surprised to hear it when I asked it—THE question: "Who is going to be *my* friend?" I wanted to know.

That was the best way I could express it. It's not that I didn't have friends. I had good relationships with the women in our church. Women of all ages. They taught me how to fry chicken and cook collard greens. They babysat our children so Harry and I could go out to dinner. We went for long walks around the community college campus, and we shared Sunday dinners together. We taught Sunday school together, and we threw baby showers together. But for me, there was something missing.

On that particular morning, the very first time I asked the question, Harry said to me, "Jesus is your friend." Even now, nearly three decades later, we both laugh at that. While he meant well, and what he said was true, it wasn't the answer I needed. No offense to Jesus.

Over the years I've asked that question many more times. I've watched my husband find fulfillment in his work as a pastor. I've seen my children make new friends and keep the old. I have cheered them on to realizing their dreams, and I have watched as they've stumbled and worked hard to chart their own course in this world. In all those years, my focus was on creating a safe place for my husband to return at the end of the day and a haven for my children to thrive in. At least, that was my goal. And while I loved my role and my work and my friends and my home, I still found myself wondering if there was more for me.

Howard Thurman is credited with giving us these wise words:

> "Don't ask yourself what the world needs. Ask yourself what makes you come alive and then go do that. Because what the world needs is people who have come alive."[3]

Let me be clear, there is much fulfillment in a good marriage and in making a home and in raising children and in putting down roots in a church congregation. All of these things are life-giving. They are beautiful, and rich, and sacred, and true. They are priceless, and my experience has been no exception. By the same token, these are not the only conditions in which to experience a life of beauty and richness, sacredness and truth. Regardless of your marital situation, your home life, your work, or your friends, life-giving experiences are all around us.

There is, however, a difference between something that gives us life—as beautiful as that may be—and a thing that makes us *come alive*. You know it when you see it.

THERE IS, HOWEVER, A DIFFERENCE BETWEEN SOMETHING THAT GIVES US LIFE—AS BEAUTIFUL AS THAT MAY BE—AND A THING THAT MAKES US COME ALIVE.

On that morning all those years ago, when I first asked my husband, "Who's going to be *my* friend?" it wasn't really friendship I was missing. *Friend* was the closest I could get to describe what I felt was absent from my life. The idea of friendship has to do with deep connectedness. If you have a good friend, you know what I mean. A good friend can help you feel anchored and grounded, but a good friend can also give you freedom and lightness. Granted, there was only a small part of me that was feeling a bit anxious and unmoored, but it kept showing up and making me pay attention to it.

A good friend can help you feel anchored and grounded but a good friend can also give you freedom and lightness.

In life, there are people and places and experiences and moments that breathe life into you. They remind you of what is good in life, and they inspire you to keep on keeping on. But there are also moments in this life—and I would imagine these moments come fewer and farther between—that awaken something in us. These moments call us to reach higher and to dig deeper. They invoke us to take a risk, to defy logic, to step into a dream that seems far-fetched. And they make us step outside of the box we've been living in.

These are burning bush moments (Exodus 3). There are Esther moments (Esther 4:14). They are the moments where we hang a scarlet cord from our window just before the battle (Josh. 2:21). They are the instances in which we commit to make "your people . . . my people, and your God . . . my God" (Ruth 1:16).

These are the moments that make us come alive. They are the moments of pushing new life into the world or holding a placard in the middle of the street in hopes of making a little bit of space for justice. They are the moments of writing a book proposal or registering an LLC. They are the moments of studying to take the GRE or trading in the corporate office for a long-term mission assignment. They are the moments of enrolling in seminary, despite homeschooling four beautiful children every day. They are the moments of stepping up to the mic for the very first time or showing up at the page in the early morning hours. These are the moments of dreams coming true.

Maybe you sense it, as I did, in the midst of your life-giving days. Perhaps you've got a small corner of your soul reminding you from time to time that God's gifts are life-giving *and* they are moments of coming alive. It's tempting to shove those feelings of *something more* to the back burner, especially for those of us who have a life that seems beautiful and rich and full of life. But may I just whisper here to you and gently say, *"Pay attention"*? And for those who feel the questioning and who might feel guilty for thinking there may be something more, don't lose heart. Be steadfast where you are and soak up the life-giving moments. But also? Surrender those questions and feelings of guilt to the God who puts the dreams in our hearts.

Psalm 27:14 (NIV) reminds us of the significance of patience as we wait for God to connect us with our *something more*:

> Wait for the LORD;
> be strong and take heart
> and wait for the LORD.

It was decades before God slowly began to reveal His plan for me as a writer, author, and speaker. During the time of waiting and wondering, my life, indeed, was full. And it was beautiful. And, truth be told, I could not have fully lived into this work—this ministry—while I had small children at home. God was getting things ready, and . . . He was getting *me* ready.

Our hearts crave connections that God longs to fulfill

Our hearts crave connections that God longs to fulfill. These connections we crave are unique to each one of us. If you find yourself wondering if there might be *something more*, don't push those feelings aside or feel guilty for sensing something more than the beautiful life you have already. Keep offering those feelings up to God. Stay focused where you are. Express your gratitude for the life-giving moments. Don't try to work something up that isn't from God, but instead, wait to see what He's got in store for you. He *will* fill the desires of your heart. He *will* make you come alive. He *will* prepare you along the way. Wait for the Lord. Be strong, take heart, and wait for the Lord.

CONNECTION QUESTIONS

1. How would you describe your season of life today?

2. Is there some beautiful thing that feels undone in your life? What is it?

3. What is the most beautiful thing about your *current* season of life? In what ways does your current season of life make you *come alive*?

CONNECTION CHALLENGE

Ask God to open your eyes to His plan for the day or this season. As you seek God's agenda over your own, ask Him to reveal to you the ways He hopes to bless you and strengthen you in the waiting.

Write down some of the lessons you've learned while waiting in the past so that in your present you can more clearly see God at work.

PRAYER

Jesus, it is in You that we live, move, and have our being. Thank You for making us come alive. Thank you for abundant life. Give me patience in the waiting. Give me focus in this current season. Help me to trust Your timing and direction for what lies ahead. As I eagerly anticipate the gifts of the future, please don't let me miss the beauty that surrounds me—right here, right now. Amen.

Making Peace with Jealousy

CONSIDER

Make peace with jealousy by actively capturing thoughts, being willing to seek forgiveness, and creating a Truth-filled reality.

> "For where envy and selfish ambition exist, there is disorder and every kind of evil. But the wisdom from above is first pure, then peace-loving, gentle, compliant, full of mercy and good fruits, without favoritism and hypocrisy. And the fruit of righteousness is sown in peace by those who cultivate peace."
>
> JAMES 3:16–18

ENGAGE

Practice actively capturing your thoughts as you go about your day.

I grew up with the privilege of attending a swanky private school in Dallas, Texas. My friends were the daughters and sons of high-powered politicians, well-known doctors, and struck-it-rich oil people. They lived in mini-mansions in the best parts of the city. Their bedrooms were big, filled with the latest, trendiest toys, and don't get me started about the clothes in their closets. All the brand names you could imagine.

I didn't attend this school because I was in *that* club. My parents were school teachers, and I was given a teacher discount to attend. We lived in a sweet little house in a basic part of town. I had a closet of handmade or consignment store clothes, and my toys were things I invented from cardboard boxes or art supplies. While I had more than I needed, my kid mind could only see *all* that my friends had. I was jealous of things like extravagant birthday parties, Guess jeans, and cars with seat heaters. Yes, in 1980 that was a BIG deal.

We see through Scripture that jealousy is human: Cain and Abel, Sarah and Hagar, Rachel and Leah, Saul and David, and Martha and Mary. This list could keep going. James 3:15 goes so far as to say that jealousy is "unspiritual" and "demonic." Wow. That terrifies me. How about you?

How do you define jealousy? My definition is pretty simple.

Jealousy: desiring something that someone else has, to the point of stirring up negative emotions in my heart and mind

The truth is I have jealous thoughts every day. I see the Pinterest pin of someone's perfectly put-together playroom and I think, "If only I had more money! I could totally do that too." I see the Instagram post of someone's art and I think, "If only I had more time. I would make an awesome artist, and then I could rock my Instagram posts." I see the Facebook post where someone inked a three-book deal with an incredible publishing house, and I think, "Why can't that be me?" I see the announcement about the latest speaker line-up for a conference I love, and I think, "Hey! Don't you see me over here? What makes them better than me?"

Jealousy is foul and hurtful, and it lives in me. Does it live in you?

Does jealousy live in you?

The question becomes what do we do with this reality? How do we prevent jealousy from seeping into us? How do we halt the green-eyed monster from destroying a fulfilling relationship with God and others?

James 3:16 (VOICE) says, "Any place where you find jealousy and selfish ambition, you will discover chaos and evil thriving under its rule." This sense of disorder isn't necessarily external but actually resides internally.

Author John Ortberg says, "The soul seeks God with its whole being. Because it is desperate to be whole, the soul is God-smitten and God-crazy and God-obsessed. My mind may be obsessed with idols; my will may be enslaved to habits; my body may be consumed with appetites. But my soul will never find rest until it rests in God."[4]

Knowing that my soul seeks God, yet my humanness can lead me down a road of jealousy, what's a girl to do?

James 3:17–18 (ESV) goes on to say, "But the wisdom from above is first pure, then peaceable, gentle, open to reason, full of mercy and good fruits, impartial and sincere. And a harvest of righteousness is sown in peace by those who make peace."

If I take a step back and think about the nature of my envy from God's perspective, I get sick to my stomach. The more I think about it, the more I realize that having jealous thoughts is like spitting in God's face. It is my way of telling God that all that He has given me isn't enough. To think that I have been slighted, in any way, by the Maker of Heaven and Earth is a sin.

I believe what Scripture says. James 1:17 (NIV): "Every good and perfect gift is from above, coming down from the Father of the heavenly lights, who does not change like shifting shadows." God isn't up in heaven treating us like dogs who have to perform for treats. We are His children. We are *on purpose.*

WE ARE HIS CHILDREN. WE ARE ON PURPOSE.

What I have and who I am is not an accident, it is not haphazard, and it is a gift from a loving God. If I believe that to be true, then I have to trust that the gifts and opportunities given to me are uniquely mine. I need to stop lusting after someone else's successes or things that have been created just for them. But all of that is easier said than done, right?

Just because we understand jealousy to be part of our human nature doesn't make it acceptable. How do I live something different so that I am not reaping the consequences of the seeds sown by our biblical patriarchs and matriarchs?

If jealousy creates chaos and disorder, then what is the opposite of that? James says it: purity, peace, gentleness, openness, mercy, and sincerity (James 3:17). Our freedom comes by cultivating a spirit of peace, and I am thankful that is something I can obtain through the power of the Holy Spirit that lives in me.

So I have created a helpful way to remember how to live in that peace: The ABCs of Making Peace with Jealousy.

1. Actively Capture My Thoughts

"Do not conform to the pattern of this world, but be transformed by the renewing of your mind. Then you will be able to test and approve what God's will is—his good, pleasing and perfect will." (Rom. 12:2 NIV)

While my fleeting "I wishes" through the day may seem harmless, I know they aren't. Every time I allow myself to think a jealous thought, I am training my mind to believe it as reality. The more thoughts I allow to sneak in like that, the easier it becomes to be in a constant state of discontent. What can seem like silly jealousies add up and create a heart in disarray, rather than a soul that rests in thankfulness.

We recently moved from Phoenix, Arizona, to the Denver, Colorado, area. I had lived in my Arizona house for over five years, and I loved it. I was happy and comfortable there. It wasn't perfect, but it was mine and I had it decorated in ways that brought me joy. We decided to buy a fixer-upper in Colorado partly because the cost of living is higher, and partly because we wanted to make something our own. But the day we took ownership of the "new" house, I was a total grump. With every turn I made, all I saw was a disaster that was never going to be okay. I could see zero good in our home!

That complaining outlook oozed out from me and onto my family. I was short in my tone, filled with a negative attitude, and quick to remind my husband that this dissatisfaction was all his doing. U G L Y!!! It took me days before I came down from my high horse. But when I did, I realized I had to capture the negative thoughts and remind myself that I am thankful to have a roof, a house with heat and walls, a bed to sleep in, and a family I love. Choosing better thoughts doesn't make the house stop being a renovation train-wreck—it still is—but it does allow me to override the negative feelings with a God-centered attitude. If you were in my house with me right now, and you listened very closely, you would hear me whispering to myself, "Walls, roof, heat, and family. Walls, roof, heat, and family." Talking to myself is just one way

I capture my thoughts. What is a way you can capture your thoughts today?

2. Be Willing to Seek Forgiveness

> "If we say we have no sin, we deceive our-selves, and the truth is not in us. If we confess our sins, he is faithful and just to forgive us our sins and to cleanse us from all unrighteous-ness. If we say we have not sinned, we make him a liar, and his word is not in us." (1 John 1:8–10 ESV)

As a Christian life coach, I have the honor of enter-ing into women's stories every day. People don't get a life coach because their world is a bed of roses. It is typically because they are feeling stuck in one way or another. As I listen to each woman and their desire for change, I hear words like guilt, fear, worry, shame, doubt, com-parison, and weariness. Once we take a step back and evaluate these emotions from God's perspective we can see a clear path out, and that path involves an honest confession to God of the sin involved. This is one step toward freedom.

As a child I understood sin as something big, bad, and terrible. Things that would get you thrown in jail, like murder or stealing. As an adult, I have come to appreciate that *sin is anything that separates us from God*. Anything! Yes, that even means the thoughts and emotions that hold us in a frozen position. God has us here on this earth to live an abundant life. He sees us as the hands and feet of Christ; and we can't be that apart from Him. If we are walking in separation from God, then it is our job to repent, literally to *turn toward God* in our minds and souls. We have to remember that God is

God and stop relying on our own strength. We can't just give it lip service. Repenting has to be a heart moment.

For me, repentance happens most effectively through journaling. I write God a letter confessing the ways my heart wants control, perfection, and excess, and the ways I have plotted and schemed to get it. I expose all the sin to light and leave nothing hidden. As I write, I hand it over to God (palms open), I invite the Holy Spirit in to bring peace, and I give thanks to Jesus Christ for the sacrifice He made on the cross so that I can enjoy this renewed connection between me and God.

If you find yourself lacking connection in your relationships due to jealousy, then I urge you to carve out time and space to go to God with an honest, "I'm sorry." Allow His loving, grace-filled arms to wrap around you like a warm blanket and remind your heart that He sees you, knows you, and calls you His child.

3. Create a Truth-Filled Reality

> "My heart is not proud, LORD, my eyes are not haughty; I do not concern myself with great matters or things too wonderful for me. But I have calmed and quieted myself, I am like a weaned child with its mother; like a weaned child I am content. Israel, put your hope in the LORD both now and forevermore." (Ps. 131:1–3 NIV)

I don't think any of us wake up in the morning choosing to be jealous. Instead, jealousy seeps into the crevices of our minds like an undetected deadly poison. It seeks to destroy us and our relationships with others. But one of the most beautiful things about God is that He has not left us here on earth to battle this or any other sin alone. After Jesus went to heaven, God sent us a helper in the Holy Spirit. The life-changing power of the Holy Spirit resides in us. We have been given the fruits of the Holy Spirit, one of which is peace (Gal. 5:22–23). If we desire to live life in a state of peace, then we are required to grip and grab hold of truth. This is a choice. It is a hard choice, but it is one that is worth the fight.

TRUTH: "For to set the mind on the flesh is death, but to set the mind on the Spirit is life and peace" (Rom. 8:6 ESV).

If my goal is to create thoughts centered on peace rather than disorder, then I must saturate myself with truth from God around this concept. The practical way I make this happen is with my phone. I have decided that technology can either be used for good or evil, and I am going to use it for good. Every two hours starting at 8:00 a.m. my phone reminds me of Scripture such as:

TRUTH: And the peace of God, which surpasses all understanding, will guard your hearts and your minds in Christ Jesus (Phil. 4:7 ESV).

Or it might be a truth statement that draws me to Scripture, like "Peace. Be Still."

As the reminders go off every two hours, I read them, maybe even re-read them and, if I happen to be struggling in the moment, I will stop and pray. This process has kept my emotions from getting the better of me each day, and it keeps me grounded in a God-sized reality rather than swimming helplessly in culture-driven chaos.

The phone has become my tool for creating a truth-filled reality, but what would work for you? Is it covering your walls with Scripture art, using erasable markers to write on your mirror, or maybe Post-it notes tacked to your steering wheel and microwave? Perhaps you can try a few ways and see which one is the tool for you. The important part is making a choice to engage the power of truth and the Holy Spirit as an active and minute-by-minute part of your day.

I wish I could promise you that implementing these ABCs would prevent you from experiencing jealousy ever again, but I can't. What

I can assure you is that by actively capturing your thoughts, seeking forgiveness, and living a life saturated in truth, you will deepen your relationship with God. Walking more closely with God will help your soul remember that you are loved, you are His workmanship, and you have a value in this world that can never be compared to another's.

CONNECTION QUESTIONS

1. What—or who—were your last jealous thoughts about?

2. What words jump off the page for you when you read James 3:17–18?

3. If you were able to have coffee with God, how do you think He would speak over your life about jealousy?

CONNECTION CHALLENGE

One of the most effective ways to combat envy is with encouragement. It isn't often easy, but take some time to think of people who have stirred up jealousy in you and make the choice, instead, to think about how your life has been grown by them.

Practice actively capturing your thoughts as you go about your day. When envious thoughts sneak in, capture them and replace them with encouragement. When negative words threaten to tumble out, consider how to flip them to a positive. Ask God to help you identify the thoughts that He wants to replace with His truth.

PRAYER

God, we are thankful for Your love and how it extends over us, even in the places we are weak. We desire for our souls to live connected with You. And we know that walking closely with You isn't feasible if jealousy is creating a barrier between us. Stir up in us the motivation to replace our jealous thoughts with ones of truth and peace. We trust that as we draw nearer to You a fresh sense of freedom will arrive. Amen.

"I Am with You . . ."

Knowing God makes being known by others possible and beautiful.

"Fear not, for I am with you; be not dismayed, for I am your God; I will strengthen you, I will help you, I will uphold you with my righteous right hand."

ISAIAH 41:10 (ESV)

ENGAGE

Invite a friend over for coffee and choose a verse to memorize together, one that reminds you of God's "withness" in the middle of your circumstances.

By Stacey Thacker

Sometimes fear shows up like an uninvited house guest on our doorstep with a cute little suitcase packed full of lies. Before long, without planning, we are sharing cups of hot coffee, swapping stories, letting fear feel quite at home. She has a way about her that says, "Trust me, I'm your friend." She even puts her arm around us and tells us we have every right to be afraid. Fear understands us. Fear wants to spend time with us. Fear prefers us. And suddenly that suitcase full of lies finds its way not just into our homes but our hearts as well.

I wish I could tell you I wasn't speaking from experience on the matter. Honestly, the opposite is absolutely true. I've struggled with fear more than I care to admit. I remember during my sophomore year at Indiana University, a mentor said to me boldly but gently, "Fear of failure dominates your life." She went on to name a few more fears that "dominate my life" like "fear of rejection." *Ouch*. Her words shot straight to my heart with stellar precision. I sat fidgeting in my seat, realizing I had been discovered, and wondering if I should own it or not. I decided it was time to be honest with my own heart and spent the next several weeks pouring into God's Word on the subject. It was the beginning of my all-out battle to evict fear from my heart. I've made some progress in the twenty or so years since, but when something is known to "dominate your life" it doesn't go away overnight.

Fear knocks on my door regularly. When my family had moved to a new state and my husband traveled for work, I was home alone with my kids, and I was afraid. Fear also shows up anytime I'm asked to do something that might end up with me failing in front of other people, like public speaking. The truth is I need to remember that fear may be a big four-letter word, but *with* is even bigger.

God says, "Fear not, for I am with you" (Isa. 41:10 ESV).

I learned then, and remind myself frequently, the only thing that sends fear packing from the corners of my heart and home is focusing on the "withness" of my God. He exhorts me not to fear. Why? Because *elohiym*—the one true God—is with me. I love what F. B. Meyer says: "God incarnate is the end of fear; and the heart that realizes that he is in the midst . . . will be quiet in the midst of alarm."[5] Fear that begins in our mind and travels to our heart meets its match in God. He is in our midst, and His presence displaces our fear. Or at least it should in theory.

This is the best kind of news for our hearts today. Putting our faith into action and actually believing it can be difficult at times. One of my favorite authors is Amy Carmichael. She was a missionary among the poor in India. Not long after her arrival to her assignment she fell, injuring herself so severely that she spent the rest of her days bedridden. Still convinced God was working in the midst of her story, she wrote honest and beautiful words. I think she must have struggled with fear as well because her words stir my heart to trust God no matter what life has tossed my way. Her poem called "The Age-Long Minute" is such a beautiful picture of a God who is with us:

> *Thou art the Lord who slept upon the pillow*
> *Thou art the Lord who soothed the furious sea*
> *What matter beating wind and tossing billow, if only we are*
> *   in the boat with thee?*
> *Hold us in quiet through the age-long minute,*
> *while thou art silent and the wind is shrill,*
> *Can the boat sink, Lord, while thou art in it?*
> *Can the heart faint that waiteth on thy will?*[6]

I know a thing or two about age-long minutes. I'm living one right now. My daughter has been a pretty sick little girl for the majority of the past year. Last spring we landed in the hospital for eight days and left with a life-changing diagnosis. We have prayed. We have cried big ugly tears, and we have begged God to show us how to help her. He has not left us for one minute. I assure you the truth of Isaiah 41:10, His "withness," is evident. Still, watching one of your babies struggle is heart wrenching. We have been told there is no cure and our greatest hope is for seasons of remission. Of course, we know God can heal her. We would welcome it and ask for it every single day. For now, we work with doctors, take medicine, and try our best to eat better.

As a part of her journey she needs frequent tests. They are not the kind of tests I care to experience as an adult, and for a child they are pretty horrible. Every month, when test day nears I start by telling her the truth about what to expect. I tell her we need to do it because this is how we find out what is happening inside her body. I remind her of the last time we took the very same test and how God made her brave. I also promise to buy her a smoothie after it is over. Even with all of this, it is common for tears to start early in the morning of test day.

Do you think I walk her to the door of the clinic, tell her to dry her tears, and leave her there alone? Of course not. As long as I am allowed to do so, I go with her. I am present with her. I grab her hand before they call her name. I continue to speak truth over her heart. I help her. And when the time comes for the big test I don't just hold her, I get in the chair first. She sits on my lap. I wrap one arm around her shaking body, and I place my other hand on her shoulder. I pray. I keep holding her. I absorb as much of her anxiousness and tears as I am able. When the test is complete, we race off to our smoothie date and celebrate.

Does our God do any less for his daughters? He is present with us. We can climb into His lap at any time. He holds us when the storm is brewing and our hearts are tempted to give in to fear. At precisely the point where you feel everything is falling apart, He holds. And He does not stop. Not ever.

Are you in an age-long minute, too, my friend? Are you waiting for answers that seem slow to come? Are the winds raging? Do you think maybe this storm may be the final blow in a series of truly hard things? Life feels like that so much of the time. Leave it to fear to show up in that exact moment. Can I encourage your heart today? Let Jesus hold you in quiet during your age-long minute. I promise the boat will not sink and your heart will not faint because He is in it with you.

God's presence is a package deal; it always comes with a promise. Just in case, like me, fear tries to convince you she is your BFF and is reluctant to leave, God has tucked three promises tied to His presence in Isaiah 41:10.

- I will strengthen you
- I will help you
- I will uphold you

When you have the presence of God, He works to display His power on your behalf. He will strengthen you. He will help you. He will uphold you. Matthew Henry puts it like this:

> "It is against the mind of God that his people should be a timorous people. For the suppressing of fear he assures them, that they may depend upon his presence with them as their God, and a God all-sufficient for them in the worst of times. Observe with what tenderness God speaks, and how willing he is to let the heirs of his promise know the immutability of his counsel, and how desirous to make them easy: 'Fear thou not, for I am with thee, not only within call, but present with thee; be not dismayed at the power of those that are against thee, for I am thy God, and engaged for thee. Art thou weak? I will strengthen thee. Art thou destitute of friends? I will help thee in time of need. Art thou ready to sink, read to fall? I will uphold thee with the right hand of my righteousness . . . .'"[7]

Our fears may feel larger than life, but they are not larger than our all-sufficient God.

Our fears may feel larger than life, but they are not larger than our all-sufficient God who is engaged on our behalf. Whatever you might be facing today, this is truly His heart on the subject of fear: "Fear not, I am with you. I will strengthen, help, and uphold you."

God knows our hearts are forgetful and slow to believe, and within the next few verses of Isaiah 41, God puts something of an exclamation mark on the matter. Don't you just love when He does that?

> "Look, everyone who hated you and sought to do you wrong
>   will be embarrassed and confused.
>   Whoever challenged you with hot-headed bluster
>   will become as if they never were, and nevermore will be.
> You may go looking for them, but you won't find them;
>   because those who tried to fight with you will become as if
>   they never were.
> After all, it is I, the Eternal One your God,
>   who has hold of your right hand,
> Who whispers in your ear, "Don't be afraid. I will help you."
> (Isa. 41:11–13 VOICE)

God is our defender, and fear becomes as if she never was. My accuser, your tormenter, our enemy can't be found. Fear has left the building, you might say. Instead, we have the Eternal One whispering in our ears, "Don't be afraid. I will help you." When I choose to believe God's promise, it is pretty amazing how quickly fear packs her bags and runs the other direction. She really doesn't have a choice.

I think our hearts crave this connection with God. We were made for it. He knows this and yet does far more than we can ask for or imagine (Eph. 3:20). The beautiful by-product of God's presence is the possibility of community with other women. When my heart connects with God first, I no longer worry about comparison or rejection from women who might not understand my own struggles with fear. God actually draws others into my messy story because that is where the sweet spot of connection happens naturally. I have seen this over and again as we have walked this health journey with my daughter. In the early days of her illness, women all over the world were praying for us.

> GOD ACTUALLY DRAWS OTHERS INTO MY MESSY
> STORY BECAUSE THAT IS WHERE THE SWEET
> SPOT OF CONNECTION HAPPENS NATURALLY.

I read messages to my girl from as far away as New Zealand and Madagascar, from people who were willing to walk with us in the most beautiful and loving way. It would have been easier to pull the veil over our lives, believing no one would care about our family. But with God holding us, helping us, and His constant presence, we invited others into our most difficult days. Do you know what I discovered? Knowing God makes being known by others possible and beautiful. Romans 8:31 (NIV) says, "What then shall we say to these things? If God is for us, who can be against us?" Sweet sisters from the corners of the globe stood with us, not against us. We had nothing to fear because God was with us. Friends drew near. And just as He promised, our enemy fled.

Knowing God makes being known by others possible and beautiful.

CONNECTION QUESTIONS

1. If God is the end of fear, what does that mean for you?

2. What verse from Scripture can you take refuge in when you are tempted to give way to your greatest fear?

3. We all have age-long minutes. Think back to your last one—did what you feared most actually take place? What evidence do you have that God is in the boat with you?

CONNECTION CHALLENGE

Start every day connecting your heart to God. Tell Him you are thankful for His presence in your life. I find memorizing verses that counter my fear to be the key to growing in my faith. Why not start with Isaiah 41:10 and ask a friend to join you?

Invite her over for coffee and choose a verse to memorize together, one that reminds you of God's "withness" in the middle of your circumstances.

PRAYER

Lord, thank you for being the God of the age-long minute. Thank You that you hold us, You strengthen us, and You constantly whisper in our ears, "Don't be afraid." We want to be so confident in this truth that our hearts are free to connect with other sweet sisters who might need to be encouraged today as well. Draw me close to You, and if You give me the honor of sharing my heart with others, I will point to You. Amen.

When Wounds from Women Are Hard to Forgive

CONSIDER

You and I can do impossibly hard things because Jesus goes to impossibly hard lengths to help you in impossible-to-count ways.

> "Therefore, God's chosen ones, holy and loved, put on heartfelt compassion, kindness, humility, gentleness, and patience, accepting one another and forgiving one another if anyone has a complaint against another. Just as the Lord has forgiven you, so you must also forgive."
>
> COLOSSIANS 3:12–13

ENGAGE

Take some time to send the wounds from your heart into the presence of Christ.

I married my good Air Force man not long after completing my junior year of college. Just weeks after he put the ring on my finger, we put our weighted-down car in drive and left my home state of Oklahoma for another one nearly a thousand miles away. With this transition came many good-byes. I left my beloved Oklahoma State University—and my gaggle of good friends there—to complete my senior year at a new college. I don't know how many people transfer colleges their senior year, but let me tell you what I do know: it's tough. Most people in my classes already had well-established friendships, and it was hard for me to fit in and develop my own.

As hard as that was, it was even harder to hear mean-spirited, painful words that floated across the miles from an Oklahoma friend, a friend who had been a roommate and close companion of mine. All these years later, I still remember how those words hurt me deeply, especially at a time when I wondered if I was likable enough to make new friends.

Several years ago, I attended a meeting in my son's fourth-grade classroom with his teacher and another fourth-grader's mom. After opening the big swinging door of the classroom, I walked in and sat down in one of the short, plastic-backed chairs with metal legs, my knees up to my neck. I folded my hands on the table, anxious to begin the meeting. The other mom's son had repeatedly bullied my son, and while my son tried to handle the situation on his own, it soon became obvious it required parent intervention. This was our opportunity to hash things out and come to an understanding, or so I thought.

Well, we ended up coming to an "understanding" all right, but not the kind I envisioned.

The other mom kicked off the meeting by making all kinds of assumptions and accusations about our family's lifestyle. She informed me of her knowledge that my husband was in the military, *so naturally if any child around here acted like a bully, it was mine.* It soon became apparent she believed we ran our household boot camp style, spitting out brutal little bully children in the process.

She proceeded to attack the parenting skills of both my husband and me, not to mention the character of the majority of my family members. I did my best to apologize for any wrongdoing on our part, but when I tried to explain the situation from our vantage point, she mowed over my words like an industrial grass cutter. The conversation more than stung; it shocked and grieved me. Never in my life had my character (or my family's character) been so grossly misrepresented by one woman.

More recently, in a small gathering of women I'm getting to know, we were encouraged to share a bit about ourselves. The conversation turned to music and movies we enjoy, and while I relish an array of musical genres, I commented on a type of music I especially enjoy (hint: it includes Johnny Cash and Carrie Underwood). After hearing what I shared, one woman narrowed her eyes at me. I didn't think much of it till later when I mentioned how much our family enjoyed a popular book and movie series, and then the same woman mentioned that she would *never* read that series or watch those movies. She would never allow her children to either because, in her general words, *"Those books and movies are not the ways of Christ."*

My first thought: *When one is encouraged to share a little about herself on surface matters and is then judged for it, how is she supposed to feel comfortable sharing her real deal worries and fears? Or her heart's concerns?*

Afterward, I confided in one close friend, *"Ya know, being in groups of women is hard because women can be so hard on each other."*

She nodded. I sighed.

Sometimes, a big singular incident makes you wary of women. But more often, I think, it's several smaller ones smacking into you. You find yourself picking those slights and slanders up one by one with your hand and stacking them like firebricks around your heart. With one brick you say, "This will teach me not to open up to friends." And then with another you say, "Lonely is better than looking like a loser."

I know this slow hiding of a hurting heart. But I also know the protection isolation offers always comes at a heavy price: *a less-than life.* Every time I'm tempted to move in that direction—and believe me I've been tempted—I sense the Lord speaking these words to my heart,

"Child, I have more in mind for you than that."

I know this is true, but sometimes it's just plain hard to do the work of keeping your heart open to friendships. So how do we stop allowing the wounds from some women to keep us away from joyous friendship with others? How do we begin the work of healing?

Instead of building a barrier with firebricks, perhaps we build bridges with forgiveness.

Instead of shielding our hearts by hiding them, we strengthen our hearts by framing them with forgiveness offered through the love of Christ.

I glance up at our family photo hanging above the piano, the one we took when James and Ethan were five and Faith was one. We were sitting on a picnic table in the great outdoors, our young selves surrounded by yellow and red maple leaves. That photo has survived four moves, two across an ocean. The dark mahogany wood frame has protected the picture and kept it in good condition.

But it hasn't hidden it.

Forgiveness does this same work. It is the frame that shields your heart while keeping it visible.

Forgiveness does this same work.
It is the frame that shields your
heart while keeping it visible.

When I look up the original meaning of the word *forgive*, I find its counterpart in the original Greek language is *aphesis*. *Aphesis* is defined as a sending away, a letting go.[8] According to my computer's handy dandy dictionary, the definition of *forgiveness* is the action or process of forgiving or being forgiven.[9]

It helps me to think of forgiveness as a process. Colossians 3:13 tells us, "Just as the Lord has forgiven you, so you must also forgive." Every time I read that verse, I look for a clause that says "when it feels right" or "only after she says she's sorry." But there's not a single one there. God kept it simple, really, and simply commands us to forgive. So even if I'm not *feeling* forgiving, I can still take the steps God desires to *send away* my ill feelings toward someone. And this process will strengthen my heart without closing it off because it helps me choose humility over hostility.

Here are three things to keep in mind as we work through the process of forgiving those who've hurt us:

1. **Put your energy in facts not feelings.** Resist the urge to let your frustration dictate your reaction. Here is the truth: We can't give those who've hurt us what they might "deserve" because Jesus doesn't give us what we deserve. We can love and respect them because of our love and respect for Jesus. We forgive by *doing* the right thing before we *feel* the right thing. Then we wait for the feelings to catch up.

WE FORGIVE BY DOING THE RIGHT THING BEFORE WE FEEL THE RIGHT THING.

2. **Place the offenses—and your reputation—in God's hands.** This doesn't mean all careless words and actions get a pass. There are times when it's perfectly appropriate to address situations that don't sit well with you or are just plain wrong. Still, it isn't necessarily our job to address each encounter. God sees them all, and we can absolutely count on Him to make all wrongs right. Let God be in charge of our reputations. We don't need to manage people's opinions of us because His opinion of us is the only one that counts.

3. **Practice telling truth over telling people off.** *The Message* translation of Colossians 3:13 says, "Be even-tempered, content with second place, quick to forgive an offense." When I feel the urge to tell someone off because she's wounded me, I want to reverse the order of our perceived placement and put the offender in second place. But in the upside-down ways of the kingdom, I need to get comfortable in the uncomfortable position of sitting second fiddle. I need to remember sitting in second place doesn't mean the offender is top dog, but rather it's Jesus who gets that position.

In the book *What's So Amazing About Grace*, author Philip Yancey details a story occurring ten years after the end of World War II that involved a group of Polish Christians and Christians from West Germany. The West German Christians wanted to meet with the Polish Christians to ask forgiveness for what Germany did to Poland during the war. Their goal in meeting was not only to ask forgiveness, but to also begin building a new relationship.

Upon hearing the invitation, the Polish Christians were shocked silent. Finally, one spoke up, frankly stating forgiveness was impossible. How could they forgive such evil atrocities committed to their people?

Before the group discussing the potential meeting departed, they prayed the Lord's Prayer together. Here is what happened next:

> When they reached the words "forgive us
> our sins as we forgive . . ." everyone stopped
> praying. Tension swelled in the room. The

Pole who had spoken so vehemently said, "I must say yes to you. I could no more pray the Our Father, I could no longer call myself a Christian, if I refuse to forgive. Humanly speaking, I cannot do it, but God will give us his strength!" Eighteen months later the Polish and West German Christians met together in Vienna, establishing friendships that continue to this day.[10]

On my own, there's a lot I can't do and a lot I just plain don't want to do. But that's where Jesus comes in, His power filling in my gaps. When I honestly tell God I don't have it in me to forgive, He says, "That's okay, you don't have to have it in you because I gave you my Son to be everything for you."

As you strive to get from where you are to where you want to be, remember you have a Savior who is the bridge from you to the Father. Jesus will help you forgive others and frame your heart with His love. You and I can do impossibly hard things because Jesus goes to impossibly hard lengths to help you in impossible-to-count ways. By His power, you can humble yourself to forgive and enjoy a stronger heart in the process. He will help take your heart from where it is to where His is.

You and I can do impossibly hard things because Jesus goes to impossibly hard lengths to help you in impossible-to-count ways.

He will help you take the steps to forgive, the action that builds the foundation of new friendships.

Right now, I picture several gorgeous gals, women who talk affectionately about me whether I'm in front of them or not. Women who build me up as a wife and mother. Women who ask me to share about myself and listen with kindness, compassion, and grace. God has used them to heal me, to hold me . . . to frame me with His love.

I see it now, how forgiveness always leads to letting go of the *less-than* life.

And paves the way for the *more-than* life God desires for us.

CONNECTION QUESTIONS

1. How does knowing that unforgiveness severs a connection of sorts with God's best for you motivate you to take the steps necessary to forgive?

2. What steps can you take to not only forgive those who hurt you but move to bless them too?

3. How might blessing those who are difficult to forgive bless you in return?

CONNECTION CHALLENGE

Are you holding on to any wounds from women? Words or actions that are convincing you friends aren't worth the trouble? Take some time to send those wounds from your heart into the presence of Christ.

Do this by sharing them out loud with Jesus or penning them on paper. Ask God for His wisdom on how to proceed. If you need to address the issue with someone, then pray for Christ's words and actions as you do so. But if you feel Him telling you to release the wounds to His care, then trust He will get to the bottom of things better than you ever could.

PRAYER

Dear Father in heaven, thank you for sending me Jesus, the bridge from my heart to Yours. Thank you for helping me forgive even when I don't feel like it—especially when I don't feel like it. Thank you for filling in my gaps and being what I cannot. Help me to protect my heart yet keep it open by framing it with your Truth. Help me to know what words and actions to let go so I have the space and ability to hold onto the friendships You desire for me. I love You, and I place my wounds and friendship concerns in Your caring hands. In the mighty name of Jesus, amen.

I Can't Even

If I can't love the hard-to-love people around me, I'm not loving God.

"God is love, and the one who remains in love remains in God, and God remains in him. . . . We love because He first loved us."

—

1 JOHN 4:16B, 19

ENGAGE

Ask God to give you the opportunity to love someone in your community who is going through a particularly challenging circumstance.

I can't even. I literally just cannot even.

This trendy saying pops out of my mouth more times than I care to say. Sometimes it's because my kids are hilarious or adorable and I JUST CAN'T EVEN. I can't even believe how gorgeous my daughter is. I can't even understand how my son got to be so fun and funny. I can't even comprehend how their sweet faces and sweet hearts came from a holy mix of my husband and me. I can't even begin to fathom how God would put me as the mama in charge of their little lives.

I just can't even.

Sometimes, though, that "can't even" comes out because I literally cannot even deal with them for one more second. I just can't even think about having a civil word in my head, much less have one come out of my mouth. I cannot even deal with their disrespect, their disruptions, or their disregard for me and each other.

We recently moved into an apartment. It's a tiny little thing where my kids have to share a room. My newly-tween ten-year-old daughter has had a hard time learning to live in such close confines with her seven-year-old, Tigger-like brother. He's up before everyone else, singing and bouncing and begging to play pretend. She wants to curl up in her bed and read.

My husband and I just hope they stay in their room until 7:30 in the morning.

One night as my precious girl was trying to fall asleep, everything broke loose. Her patience was gone. Her senses were at high alert, and she literally *could not even* keep the covers on her bed she was so fed up with the noises coming from her only brother.

I went into the room first, full of parental wisdom and vigor. I fluffed her blankets, tried to roll over the snoring boy, and set everything to right. I gently closed the door, and within minutes she was calling out to me again full of frustration and woes.

I tried again with a little less patience to snuggle and calm and pet her to a comfortable space for sleeping. The third time she called, she was beyond herself. She was overly tired, and maybe I was too because my heart started beating fast, my stomach was in knots, I felt tension in my arms and hands, and my shoulders were taut. She complained about her bedcovers one more time, and I just couldn't even. I walked out of the door, leaving her to cry and wail for Mommy.

I looked at my husband who was at his computer and said, "She needs someone to be gentle and love her, but I can't do it." I sat down, breathing heavily, and let my husband hold her while she slept, just like when she was a baby.

It's surprising when you can't show love to someone you genuinely love. When my kids were babies, I don't think it happened often. Even in the middle of their worst tantrums and freak-outs, I loved them so much I was willing to hold and rock and nurse and do whatever it took to calm them down, show them love, and keep them happy.

> IT'S SURPRISING WHEN YOU CAN'T SHOW LOVE TO SOMEONE YOU GENUINELY LOVE.

As they've grown and become, well, real people with real desires, real thoughts, and real opinions, I find myself wondering who these small people are. How did they grow up into someone so *other*? Why can't I read their minds anymore?

My pride in motherhood takes a blow on days like those. I should be able to comfort my daughter when she is clearly upset. I should be able to help her when she is literally unable to help herself. And yet, my Self is so upset I can't show love to the fruit of my womb, the apple of my eye.

Jesus tells a story about a Jewish guy, beaten by robbers and left to die along a road. As the man is lying there, a priest walked by, maybe on his way to visit the sick or deposit his tithe at the temple. Or maybe he was out looking at God's creation and wondering at its beauty. Yet when he saw this poor guy, he kept walking.

Then a Levite walked by. He's another of the godly dudes in Jesus' time. Jesus doesn't say if the left-for-dead guy called out to him, but can you imagine if he did?

"Sir! Help me!" Cough. Wheeze. "They took my donkey! They took my clothes! My arm—I think it's broken! Help! Please!" And the Levite, full of self or hate or something, kept walking.

Finally, a Samaritan man walked up. Samaritans were hated by Jews. Good Jews spat on the ground when one was mentioned. Samaritans were not true followers of Yahweh by any measure of the Jew's standards. But what does this ungodly half-breed do?

He bandaged the man's wounds, then took him to an inn and paid for his stay and recovery. And I wonder what might have happened if that beaten and bruised man had met the Samaritan even a day before on that same road. I wonder if he would have crossed to the other side and made the sign of the evil eye. When the Samaritan nodded his head and said, "Good day!" would the Jewish man have balked and walked quickly by?

What is it that makes some people stop and bandage their enemy's wounds and others walk away from their whiny kids?

Well, I don't think it's patience. Or good parenting techniques. I don't think it's humility or lack of selfishness. Although those certainly help. It has something to do with love. Not the romantic idea of love. Or even the parent-child bond of love. I love my daughter so much my heart aches. There's something else about love I have to remember even on hard mothering days, even when I just can't even. I must remind myself of this truth: Jesus loves me.

What is it that makes some people stop and bandage their enemy's wounds and others walk away from their whiny kids?

You know the old song, right? "Jesus loves me, this I know. For the Bible tells me so."

Jesus loves *me*. Me! With my paper-thin patience, my award-winning procrastination, and my selfish behaviors.

He *loves* me. He doesn't tolerate me. He doesn't sorta recognize me when He sees me. He actually really and truly l-o-v-e-s me. He loves big enough and strong enough to die on a cross for me and then to daily support me, lead me, and speak to me.

When the disciple John wrote his account of Jesus' life (called the book of John), he refers to himself as "the disciple whom [Jesus] loved" (John 19:26). Sometimes I laugh when I read it because it sounds almost conceited. Jesus loves you best, John? You're His favorite, huh?

In fact, I think John just really recognized what Jesus' love was and meant. In a later writing (the letter called 1 John), he spends a good part of it talking about love—how God is love, how He loves us and calls us children, how we are to love others.

If you read 1 John chapters 3–4, you might get a little dizzy from the up and down, back and forth about God's love—love one another, love comes from God, love is God, love is born of God, love knows God, if you don't love you don't know God, and on and on it goes. It reminds me of the girls weaving in and out of a Maypole dance—his words spinning round and round and tightly tying up this deep description of God's love.

One sentence toward the end of the letter gets me, though. It's an oft-quoted verse, but when you read it, there are layers and meaning beneath the words. John says, "We love because He first loved us" (1 John 4:19).

Go ahead, read it again: We love because He first loved us.

I think a lot of times we read this as, "I'm only able to love because Jesus loved me first. I can only serve at the soup kitchen because Jesus enabled me to do so with His love. I can only be kind to my rude neighbor because Jesus set love into motion in the beginning. He's a good example of how to love."

I think it's more than that. *Jesus first loved us.* That's the important phrase. His deep love sent Him hurtling through time and space to be born of a virgin in a stable in Bethlehem. His strong love kept Him on a Roman cross when He could have stepped down without a word. His love rescues us, surrounds us, covers us, and holds us together.

His love rescues us, surrounds us, covers us, and holds us together.

Corrie ten Boom, a Dutch Christian who hid Jews in her home during World War II and was eventually arrested and imprisoned in a concentration camp by the Nazis, recognized this love. Two decades after her release she gave hundreds of devotional messages via radio in the Netherlands. In one of them she says, "When you throw an empty bottle in an ocean, it will immediately fill with and be surrounded by ocean water. If you throw yourself in Jesus' arms in complete surrender, you will be filled and surrounded by an ocean of God's love."[11]

Isn't that how you'd like to be loved—filled and surrounded? I'm overwhelmed and humbled and grateful at that kind of love. It's like pushing on a sore muscle—it hurts and feels good at the same time. I can't get away from the feeling and its seriousness. That knowledge changes me—it changes my view of others because I know that I'm not the only one Jesus loves. He loves the whole world with the same intensity and passion.

He wants us to jump into that ocean of love, be filled up and surrounded. And then? Like a full bottle, pour out His love on others. So when I begin to pour out love, especially when it's difficult, I'm doing it not as a random act of kindness, but as a deliberate move to engage others in the love I've experienced.

Then I am able to look at my children not as extensions of myself or little people I have to take care of—they are now children "whom Jesus loves." I don't see broken men on the side of the road and think, "Poor guy. Someone should call the homeless shelter down the street for him." I look at him and say, "He is a beloved child of God! What can I do for him?" I don't look at the moms sitting in the waiting room at ballet or in the stands at baseball and say, "Those ladies need to stop whining about their lives." I see them as precious jewels whom God is surrounding with His love.

It's about putting on love-colored glasses so you *can't even* help but love the people around you. It's feeling that breath of God on your face and wanting to breathe it out on your neighbors and friends. It's about knowing the weight of that loving finger of God on your heart and wishing everyone could know it too.

After the John-whom-Jesus-loved wrote the aforementioned, "We love because He first loved us," he said something else that kind of gives me the chills. He wrote, "If anyone says, "I love God," and hates his brother, he is a liar; for he who does not love his brother whom he has seen cannot love God whom he has not seen" (1 John 4:20 ESV).

> IT'S ABOUT PUTTING ON LOVE-COLORED
> GLASSES SO YOU CAN'T EVEN *HELP BUT*
> LOVE THE PEOPLE AROUND YOU.

If I can't love the hard-to-love people around me, I'm not loving God. What a beautiful (and hard) spiral this love thing is. Loving God and loving people is all intertwined. And I think I like that. Jesus' love for me is not so I can bottle it up and save it. It's not so I can simply enjoy it and keep it like a pet. Jesus' love for us is a beautiful gift to be shared, a present to be enjoyed by all.

He loves me. He loves you. I *can't even* not live in that love and share it with others. Especially those who call me upstairs ten times a night to fix bedcovers.

CONNECTION QUESTIONS

1. How does it make you feel to read 1 John 4:19–21, exchanging the word "brother" with the name of a hard-to-love person in your life?

2. What kind of daily reminder could you put around your home to remind yourself that Jesus loves you intimately (and loves those around you the same)?

3. What is it about God's love that gives you an "I can't even" moment?

CONNECTION CHALLENGE

Ask God to show you one person in your path you can show love to today. If you are really feeling brave, think of the one person in your daily life that is hardest for you to love, or ask God to give you the opportunity to love a woman in your community in a particularly challenging circumstance. Ask God to really help you see how much He loves that person.

Whatever you do next and however you do it, let your action be out of a clear understanding of Jesus' great love for you and for that person. Imagine the greatness that might follow—a deeper relationship with God and maybe with a new friend!

PRAYER

Heavenly Father, thank You for loving me. Thank You for LOVING ME! I am blown away by this amazing love. You are so big, so holy and so powerful—yet You are intimately in love with me. Help me put on those love-colored glasses so I can see how especially fond of others You are. I want to live and act in a way that reminds others of that love. I want to walk in step with You and love my neighbors in a way that shows them You. I love You, Jesus. I do.

Friendship . . . is born at the moment when one man says to another "What! You too? I thought that no one but myself . . ."

– C. S. LEWIS, *THE FOUR LOVES*

CONNECTING

WITH

(FRIENDS)

MORE

PURPOSEFULLY

The Gift of Imperfection

You, my friend, are not the discarded, ugly, unwanted item in the store. You are the precious, beautiful gift meant for exactly the right friends.

> "Therefore encourage one another and build each other up as you are already doing."
>
> 1 THESSALONIANS 5:11

ENGAGE

Throw the "ugly Christmas sweater" contest of crafting—best craft fail wins. Give your friends the gift of imperfection.

If I were a superhero I would have two unique skills to offer the world—the ability to find and fall in love with the most expensive item in the store, and the ability to find and model the ugliest item in the store.

I could blame it on genetics—the first skill on my mom, the second on my aunt. My mom has the most beautiful talent for spotting just the right gift for just the right person across the store. My aunt would take my twin sister and me into a store and challenge us to find the craziest outfit. The joy of this skill set is experienced by more than my aunt and sister. For the last decade or more, my family has secretly passed around a very silver, very ugly, very awkward piece of women's clothing into one another's Christmas gifts.

There is something about having an eye for the funniest, strangest, most off-the-wall items that I've accepted as a quirky part of my personality. It also makes planning events a little more fun.

A few years ago I was invited to record part of my story of friendship and community for (in)courage's "in real life" event—lovingly named (in)RL after the Internet acronym for the same phrase. For three years (in)courage invited women to share their stories, both on camera and at in-home, in-church, and in-coffee shop gatherings. It was an invitation to bring together old friends and new, to go out of our comfort zones and into a place where God could begin the work of healing and restoring the hurting parts of our hearts.

It was scary. Sharing my story of brokenness and loss was a challenge. I didn't want to admit that I was a failure at friendship, or that I had—on more than one occasion—been told, "Perhaps we just shouldn't be friends." It's hard enough to live through those moments of heartache, but to share them on video for women around the world to hear? Nervous is an understatement.

I'd spent a few years reading the words on (in)courage and realized that all of those women had invited me into their stories. It gave me hope and helped me feel brave because I knew I wasn't alone. Their courage gave me courage, and I knew, as nervous as I was, that God had invited me to share in a safe space. I had read dozens of real-life, messy stories on those online pages and knew I wasn't alone.

There is something so beautiful that happens when we give each other the gift of imperfection. When we have the courage to go first and bravely share our messy parts, it invites others to share theirs. When we stop building a wall around our hearts and instead we crack open the door to let others see inside, what they'll find isn't irreparably damaged, but tender and vulnerable. And in those moments, when our story is out there for someone else to hear, and they peek in, look around, and say "me, too"—healing begins.

> WHEN OUR STORY IS OUT THERE FOR SOMEONE ELSE TO HEAR, AND THEY PEEK IN, LOOK AROUND, AND SAY "ME, TOO"—HEALING BEGINS.

So I sat in front of those cameras with a spotlight in my face and shared my story. It was a story of a shy girl who never quite knew how to make friends unless they lived inside a book. A girl who sheltered her heart with a wall of bitterness, regret, and a desperate need to be noticed, which led to a series of my own mistakes. I didn't know how to be a friend, but I expected everyone around me to be a great one. When others failed my exceptionally high expectations, I shut down. Instead of finding ways to build others up and encourage them, I ran away, and then was hurt when those friends didn't fight for me.

In that video I shared that even a decade later, I was afraid of community. Can you imagine? Here I was, sharing a story that was supposed to encourage women to be in community, and I was afraid of starting my own outside of the one God had allowed me to build online. The irony was not lost on me that God asked me to share those stories at an event that encouraged, of all things, community.

It was even more ironic that I would feel led to host an in real life gathering of friends—and strangers who would become friends—to watch those (in)RL videos. There is nothing quite like baring your heart to a camera and then to sit in a room and watch other people watch your story unfold. But I knew I was supposed to be brave, so I put on my big girl pants and gathered a few close friends to help with the planning.

We'd chat online in the evenings after our children were all in bed, deciding who would host (my home was too small; another friend lived too far away), what food to bring (you can never go wrong with some kind of dip and a lot of chocolate), and determining the plan for when we weren't watching the videos.

Inevitably, we would end up on Pinterest, with the best intentions of finding easy, meaningful, fun activities for all levels of crafty experience. The responsible ones in the group would add cute ideas to our Pinterest board while I went in search of what anyone with my particular skill set would find: the most ridiculous craft ideas ever to grace the Internet.

We laughed until tears rolled down our cheeks at yarn-covered alpaca pin cushions, toilet paper roll earrings, and flower pots with our faces on them (the plant would grow and be our hair). It turned into a contest to see who could find the silliest craft idea—the alpaca won, after much debate about whether it was a llama or alpaca, or if it really mattered if it was wearing a sombrero.

In the end we didn't make any of those crafts. But I learned to take friendship—and myself—a little less seriously through those late-night conversations. I'd assumed for so long that to have meaningful connections with other women we needed to talk about important topics all the time, dig deep into serious conversations, and cry more than we laughed. I would often walk away from a day out with friends feeling like I'd failed because we stayed on the surface of our responses to "How are you?" I struggled to believe that fun was a valuable resource in friendship. But my community in those planning meetings was built on fun and trust, and we encouraged one another to be brave and try new things.

It was through laughter that we built shared memories and experiences, and that laughter spilled over to our gathering. While my expectations were for a serious, formal event where we would share our deepest heart secrets and cry as we prayed with and for one another, the reality was even more beautiful. Our laughter and fun over failed attempts at craft projects and the imperfect parts of life helped us relax as we settled in to watch those videos. Some of us had only met that day, but as we sat on sofas and ate snacks, the laughter we shared opened our hearts to receive the stories we were hearing.

We saw ourselves in those stories of friendship and community. And our own stories were shared.

Arthur Ashe once said, "Start where you are. Use what you have. Do what you can." That's what we did. We embraced where we were—new friends or old, serious or lighthearted. We used our stories and our words to affirm friendships and start new ones, healing little hurts and starting the process to heal bigger ones along the way. We did what we could, where we could, with what we had. And in those few hours it was enough.

I didn't know that God would use every one of my struggles with friendship to serve Him in ministry. While I could see the benefit of using my words, it was harder to see how God could ever use my struggles for His good. I didn't know that He would soften my heart toward friendship, encouragement, and lifting others up as He brought me through a season where I needed someone to do that for me. I would have chosen myself as the messiest, strangest, ugliest thing in the room—but God saw the gift. He knew that in order for me to understand the importance of lifting up and encouraging others, I would first need to experience those things for myself. Through those experiences, I learned a few things about lifting others up and encouraging them:

Encouragement and envy can't coexist—Healthy friendships are formed when we can look past our fears and focus on how we can encourage someone else. We move from a "what's in it for me" focus and instead start to ask God to show us how we can love others in a way that honors them—and Him. When we encourage others we show them that we love THEM more than we love our own agendas. We choose to elevate people instead of our own platforms and personal agendas.

Lifting others up lifts us as well—The best leaders (and friends) are the ones who see the potential in others and help them shine in their strengths. Using our gifts to help others discover theirs sharpens everyone.

God doesn't waste any of our experiences, and He doesn't give up on us. Was I excited to go through friendship break-ups and seasons of loneliness? Not at all—and if I'm honest I'll tell you that I hope to never go through it again. But the gifts God has given me? The way He has created beauty out of the ashes? The joy found in knowing He chose to use pieces of me I would have kept hidden? They are priceless.

You, my friend are not the discarded ugly, unwanted item in the store. You are the precious, beautiful gift meant for exactly the right friends.

When we share our imperfect, messy, funny, hard, real stories with one another we invite others into our lives and take another step toward becoming the friend we wish we had. Discovering how to be the type of friend I always wanted took years. It's a continual journey. But there is an incredible amount of power in the words we use to encourage our friends and, with practice, God has developed in me a love for lifting others up.

He'll do that for you, too, you know. Maybe you're reading this and you're tired of being the planner, the inviter, the includer, the fixer, the organizer, the adult. I've been there. I've wanted to run away and avoid community. I've been tired of the hard work it takes and tired of constantly protecting my heart. But when we focus on what we can gift to others with our words and our stories the way Scripture asks us to do, God will bless our efforts. Eventually we'll count ourselves among the last part of that verse in 1 Thessalonians 5:11: "as you are already doing."

You, my friend, are not the discarded, ugly, unwanted item in the store. You are the precious, beautiful gift meant for exactly the right friends. You are chosen and loved, cherished and valued. The experiences you've had and the heartache you've gone through can be used to lift someone else up. Turn your hurts into something that helps and, along the way, know that laughing is a valuable gift.

CONNECTION QUESTIONS

1. When was the last time you laughed with friends?

2. How have you seen God redeem your past friendship hurts?

3. How has encouragement changed your experience as a friend?

CONNECTION CHALLENGE

Intentionality is key when planning time with friends. Work, home, and life can take over. And before you know it, you've gone months without experiencing the joy of friendship. Make this a priority for you and your girlfriends.

Invite friends to make a craft before coming and bring the finished product. Consider it the "ugly Christmas sweater" contest of crafting—best craft fail wins. Give your friends the gift of imperfection—and laughter.

PRAYER

Father, help us to find joy in our friendships. Thank You for the gift of laughter that opens doors to heal hearts, and thank You for never wasting a single one of our experiences. We pray for a glimpse of Your plan and purpose for our stories. Give us the courage to lift one another up and encourage those around us with love, laughter, and the gift of imperfection.

Lantern Lights

CONSIDER

Become a city on a hill, a light and beautiful and inviting experience amidst a world that seems to love the dark.

"You are the light of the world. A city situated on a hill cannot be hidden. No one lights a lamp and puts it under a basket, but rather on a lampstand, and it gives light for all who are in the house. In the same way, let your light shine before men, so that they may see your good works and give glory to your Father in heaven."

MATTHEW 5:14–16

ENGAGE

Share a funny story and give yourself permission to send some of those cares and burdens to God, floating like lanterns on the waves of your laughter.

By Annie F. Downs

I love the scene in *Tangled* when Rapunzel and Flynn Rider are out in the boat and the sky fills with Chinese lanterns. The dark night fills with firefly-like lights, and the sky turns from black to a really peaceful dark blue, almost purple, as the yellow-hued lanterns float upward.

They are everywhere. Floating up from the castle, then down over the lake, the specks of light work together to form a totally new color of night. They make it seem magical, not dark.

Do you remember that part of the movie? It's almost breathtaking, even as a cartoon. The amount of lanterns in the sky, around the little boat holding the two main characters, makes for what I consider the most beautiful moment in the film. (There are multiple yearly celebrations around the globe where you can see these lanterns launched *en masse*, the most well-known one being in Thailand.)

Obviously, after seeing the movie and doing some research online of my own, I wanted to send up Chinese lanterns in my neighborhood with my friends. We don't have a castle or a canoe, but we would figure out a way around that. I ordered lanterns off the Internet, and the box showed up on my doorstep thanks to the kind mailman. The lanterns came in a pack of ten, so I ordered two packs. According to the illustrated directions, they seemed simple enough—take them out of the package, flatten them out, light the fueled rice paper ring on the base, and in no time they will float away and you'll be surrounded by the beauty of a Disney film. (Or so we thought.)

With twenty to launch, my buddies spread out across a field by my house and got ready to light. At the same time, we set lit match to ring of future fire and waited.

And waited.

And waited.

We each held a lantern and watched impatiently as they lit up but never floated away. We tried throwing them, we tried lifting our hands above our heads, hoping a few more inches skyward would bring takeoff.

It didn't happen. Fifteen minutes into the event, we were acting ridiculous. Running like our fire-lit lanterns were kites that needed wind to pick up, throwing them back and forth while trying to avoid getting burned, and eventually just sitting on the ground with our lit lanterns in hand, gripped by an edge of the paper lantern, laughing at the idea of what we imagined versus what we actually got.

The memory is still great. It is one of those running inside jokes, and we laugh about it often. If something goes wrong, if our expectations aren't met, if we have to laugh off something to keep from crying, someone will usually say, "Today deserves some Chinese lanterns."

Jesus talks about light in Matthew 5:14–16:

"You are the light of the world. A town built on a hill cannot be hidden. Neither do people light a lamp and put it under a bowl. Instead they put it on its stand, and it gives light to everyone in the house. In the same way, let your light shine before others, that they may see your good deeds and glorify your Father in heaven" (NIV).

I picture that same hue as the Chinese lanterns, the warm glowing yellows that only come from real fire, contained in small quantities.

In 2014 I visited Israel for the first time and walked up the Mount of Beatitudes to where Jesus preached these exact words to a crowd gathered near Him. I saw how, as you look across the terrain of that area, you can see little patches of homes, little cities literally built on the sides of hills. And I imagined, in that moment, what it was like to see them at night. That same yellow hue of candlelight in homes, clustered together to form a community, just like I imagined those lanterns in the sky. I thought about the friendships in those towns, thousands of years ago, and how Jesus knew those villages.

It feels like He wasn't just asking us to be a light, to stand bright and alone like a lighthouse. I don't even think He was saying for us to be a lamp, necessarily. When I picture this scene He's describing, I picture a group of women sitting around, after the chores were finished for the day, laughing and reminiscing by candlelight. Because the lamp isn't hidden under a bowl, it lights the whole house, giving light to everyone gathered there. It's inviting. It's welcoming. It's friendly.

Let your light shine.

Let your light shine so others see your good deeds—light your candle, set it on the table, and invite some people to sit around it with you. Feed them. Laugh with them. Become a city on a hill, a light and beautiful and inviting experience amidst a world that seems to love the dark.

My group of girlfriends in Nashville got together a few weeks ago on a Sunday night for dinner. It's rare we are all available on the same night, but the stars aligned and we gathered around grilled fish and seasoned vegetables. Ten of us crowded around one table, and because the weather was still mild, we ate with the back doors open to the deck. Strung across the deck were beautiful twinkly lights, and so we turned off the lights in the dining room, lit some candles, and scattered them down the table.

We ate slowly. No one had anywhere else to be. We could see each other fine, thanks to the candles and the twinkly lights outside, and something about the shade of the meal made everyone relax and not wish to be anywhere else.

We laughed. A lot. From a haircut mishap to missing a flight (and yes, the Chinese lantern tale was retold in full), we swapped stories for hours, nibbling as we went, passing cookies when the dinner was finished. No one wanted to move at the risk that one simple trip to the bathroom could break the loveliness that had fallen over the night.

In a way I don't know how to put words around, our laughter lit up the night too. That seems true to me a lot—that laughter brings light to dark places and dark moments. Something happens to my insides when a hard experience has a lifting moment of laughter—I feel resettled, I feel understood, I feel relief. We need that, don't we? I think it is why grieving families sometimes break into fits of laughter that cannot be controlled. It's why one of the first things a kid learns at church is how to stifle a giggle explosion during the preaching. (And seriously, isn't that one of the very best feelings? Laughing when you aren't supposed to be laughing?) Friends who connect with you there, in that place of pure laughter and joy, are often the same ones who can dig in with you when things aren't okay. Because they know how to laugh and love when things are easy and light, they often know how to do that well in the dark also.

LAUGHTER BRINGS LIGHT TO DARK
PLACES AND DARK MOMENTS.

I saw it clearly that night, as we just kept hearing one story after another. There were also moments of deep conversation, sadness, concerns expressed. We ebbed and flowed, as happens in life often, from the serious to the hilarious. The candles melted down and puddled wax on the linen tablecloths, and the yellow hue of the light deepened. But no one moved, and the light in the room never dimmed. No dishes were rushed to the sink, no glasses loaded in the dishwasher. We just kept talking, laughing, relaxing into a place where nothing was hurried and no one was on their phones—and this was exactly where we all wanted to be.

It was just us around a table with happy hearts and candlelight.

That night made me want to reject electricity at meals all together and just have candles to light the way to dessert. The simplicity of it made the beauty of our friendship stand out, and the problems that separate us or the issues that keep us busy in our own lives all just sort of faded into the dark parts of the room. It made me think of my circle of friends who waited patiently by the same shade of light for a collection of Chinese lanterns to launch. And it made me think of the groups of women, who for hundreds and thousands of years, have sat together under that same light. I bet they laughed like we do (at the right times AND at the wrong times). I bet they had nights that they hoped would never end and chores they pushed aside.

It made me think of Israel, historically and also in the modern time where the Sabbath meal is still weekly celebrated in Jerusalem. And it made me think of Jesus.

When I read His words from Matthew, that dinner, my friends, groups of women through all of time, come to mind. Maybe that's what Jesus was talking about. He wants us to be friendly and inviting and full of life, like a city full of warmth and hubbub and laughter and love, each home inviting with the candlelight of generations gone by.

The Chinese lanterns did finally take off that night, by the way. After sitting on the field and just having them light our conversation, one gently lifted off, just hovering a few inches above the grass. You should have seen the looks on our faces. It was like a little miraculous light moment to watch that lantern make a move to float on its own power. While we were slack-jawed about that one getting its float on, another one took flight. And one after another, they began to fly. It took about twenty minutes from when we first gave up hope to when they actually floated skyward. (Lesson learned. It takes a bit of time for the lanterns to take flight.)

The sky didn't massively change colors for us like it does in the movies. Apparently it takes a few thousand to get that kind of result. (Lesson learned. It takes just a few more lanterns than we had that night.) But we did watch our twenty lanterns float up, higher in the sky than we even imagined they would go. Then we saw them spread out over the crest of the tree line, almost roll over the tops of the trees like a wave of yellow joy, and disappear out of sight. They finally flew, finally lived up to their reason for being, and brought us tons of laughs.

And that's the part that felt so magical and so full of light. I will never forget it. I had worn my rain boots, the blue ones I bought that time in New York City, more because they were by the back door when we were ready to leave than because the ground was wet or muddy. I had pulled them off when we sat around on the ground and laughed with our lanterns in hand. Those lanterns, once skybound, weren't all that illuminating for us, but the laughter and the friendship—that's the light that filled up my soul.

We watched the lanterns until they were over that crest and out of view, and then I slid my boots back on and we all turned and headed toward home. But that yellow color of the lit lanterns came with me, in my memory, in my heart.

CONNECTION QUESTIONS

1. What would it look like for your home to be a city on a hill?

2. Who in your life feels like a light in the darkness?

3. What's one of your favorite memories, whether things went exactly as planned or not, with your best friends?

CONNECTION CHALLENGE

How has laughter brought light to your life? Do you need to add a little light to a dark season? Invite a few friends over for dinner, light the candles, turn on the twinkly lights, and laugh together.

Share a funny story and give yourself permission to send some of those cares and burdens to God, floating like lanterns on the waves of your laughter.

PRAYER

God, You are light. Thank You for letting us reflect specks of Your light into the lives of the people we know. Open our eyes to see the beautiful moments all around us, the funny and the sweet and the kind, and help us to invite others into those places of light. Make our lives and our homes cities on a hill.

Kindred Souls

Deep and lasting connections aren't about geography but about what's in our hearts.

"When David had finished speaking with Saul, Jonathan committed himself to David, and loved him as much as he loved himself."

———

1 SAMUEL 18:1

ENGAGE

Spend some time investing in the friendships God has given you.

By Tonya Salomons

S he lives in California. I live in Eastern Canada. To say there is distance separating us would be a 2200-mile understatement. But for some reason it doesn't seem to matter. Kim is always there for me. She'll text me out of the blue, or leave me a congratulatory voice mail when something awesome happens in my life. We are each other's cheerleader over social media as we watch our lives unfold over the pixels on our phones and computers.

While the texts and the calls and Facebook encouragement bring me the greatest joy, it doesn't come close to describing our friendship. It's like she knows me beyond what I know about myself. It's like God knit our hearts together. It's like He planted homing beacons in the bottom of our souls, and when the going gets tough we can wade through the noise of this world with words that soothe and massage over the weariness of life events.

The last time I saw her—the last time I breathed the same air as her—was almost four years ago. God was calling me to make some big changes in my life, and I was scared out of my mind. I boarded a plane and flew those 2200 miles to California, hoping that God would make my next step clear. My friend opened the door of her home and gave me space to wrestle with the idea that God's plans for my life exceeded anything I could have ever imagined.

She didn't sit me down for a long, drawn-out conversation; she didn't ply me with countless hours of advice; she simply asked, "What do you need?" When I responded with, "I need some space to think and someone to tell me that God has my life in His hands," she hugged my neck and threw me the keys to her car and a map to get to the Pacific Coast Highway. It was in that car, with the warmth of the sun on my arms and the wind moving through my hair, that I truly understood the gift of this woman in my life.

There is another friendship that can be found in the pages of history. One that echoes holy and ancient and when I recall their story I am reminded of my own friendship with Kim. David and

Jonathan were more than just acquaintances. The Bible recounts the first time they meet in 1 Samuel 18:

"As soon as he had finished speaking to Saul, the soul of Jonathan was knit to the soul of David, and Jonathan loved him as his own soul" (v. 1 ESV).

In the verses previous to this, David had just finished slaying the Philistine, Goliath. He was summoned by Saul and identified himself as the son of Jesse. Jonathan—son of the king—was present for this conversation. When I take some time to think about that, I'm struck by how different Jonathan and David really were: David, the son of a farming man, and Jonathan, heir to a royal bloodline. In those ancient times this friendship would have been considered an impossibility. But that didn't seem to matter to either one of them. They felt a kinship with one another that transcended their stations in life.

You see, while this story happens after David defeats Goliath with nothing but a slingshot and a stone, there is another moment that is often forgotten when people talk of the connection between David and Jonathan. Did you know that Jonathan also had his moment with the Philistines? Just as David girded himself with the fear of the Lord and killed Goliath with a single stone, Jonathan also relied on God's might when he scaled a cliff with his armor bearer and took out a group of Philistines encamped at the top, sending the rest of the army into a panic. Perhaps it was David's sense of fearlessness rooted in his faith that drew his soul to Jonathan's, a sense of kindred-ness and camaraderie.

The Bible describes their souls being knit together, but beyond the poetry of their meeting it is the verses following that have me humbled by grace and commitment.

"Then Jonathan made a covenant with David, because he loved him as his own soul" (v. 3 ESV).

It seems so backward. From what we know about covenants and allegiance, David should have been the first to make a pact with Jonathan. Jonathan was a prince and David just a lowly farmer. We don't know why Jonathan acted in the moment, but perhaps he had a deeper understanding of God's plans. Maybe Jonathan knew his father's reign would not be passed down to him. Maybe Jonathan recognized the pull of eternity and knew that salvation would come out of the "stump of Jesse." What we do know for sure is that Jonathan committed himself to David and loved David as he loved himself.

And what he does next is remarkable: as a show of commitment to David, he relinquished his robe and his armor.

"And Jonathan stripped himself of the robe that was on him and gave it to David, and his armor and even his sword and his bow and his belt" (v. 4 ESV).

Some commentaries would suggest this was a symbolic act. Jonathan's robe and armor would have been an indication of his birthright. By giving these items to David, it may have appeared as if he was abdicating his right to the throne. Beyond the symbolism, however, it was a demonstration by Jonathan to David that their kinship and connection was the most important element of their relationship.

> THE SOUL OF JONATHAN WAS KNIT
> TO THE SOUL OF DAVID, AND JONATHAN
> LOVED HIM AS HIS OWN SOUL.

Remember, Jonathan was the instigator in this relationship. He was the one who cultivated and compelled their relationship to move beyond mere acquaintance. In every interaction following their initial meeting, Jonathan humbled himself below the station into which he was born and committed himself to a life of humbly serving and protecting David. It was as if each time they were together, Jonathan removed his armor all over again. This level of commitment and grace saved David's life on more than one occasion.

In all of the translations that describe David and Jonathan's relationship, there are three themes that emerge:

1. The bond was immediate.
2. The love was deep and selfless.
3. A covenant was made.

I wouldn't presume to draw exact parallels between their relationship and my own relationship with Kim, but I do see how these themes have been part of our friendship.

We are both incredibly busy women. We both have commitments to family and careers that take up the majority of our time. The fact that we live on opposite sides of the continent and in different countries would make a friendship seem impossible. While we live miles apart now, it wasn't always that way. In fact, in our younger years we went to the same church, but we seemed to run in different circles. It was about five years ago that we attended the same event while she was in town visiting family. The connection we felt toward each other in that moment was immediate, and we both made a choice to let our hearts be drawn together.

It takes strength to enter into a deep relationship with another person at the best of times, but making that kind of commitment to another person knowing they live so far away speaks to the longing we all have to be in community. It also speaks to the ability to have deep and lasting connections that aren't about geography, but about what's in our hearts.

It also speaks to the ability to have deep and lasting connections that aren't about geography, but about what's in our hearts.

When I read over the stories of David and Jonathan's friendship, they didn't do a lot of casual "hanging out." David was on the run from Saul, and a lot of that time was spent hiding in caves. That meant David and Jonathan spent very little time in each other's company, but that didn't stop them from expressing their love for one another when given the chance. When Jonathan died, David lamented his passing calling him "my brother Jonathan" and David also recognized how much Jonathan had given up in being committed to him— "Your love to me was extraordinary" (2 Sam. 1:26 ESV).

Kim and I are very different people. We come from different backgrounds. We grew up in a set of very different circumstances. Even now our lives are different; I am a student, and she is a career woman. I am an empty-nester, and she is raising a seven-year-old daughter. From the outside looking in, it would perhaps appear as if our friendship was highly improbable. Despite this, however, we saw that we needed each other and that our love of Christ and desire to be committed to His purpose would be what linked us together.

I often go back to that time in California, that time when God gave me a friend to look me in the eye and ask me what I needed. I can see more clearly now how God put Kim in my life to demonstrate to me how much

I am loved. I can see now how Kim answered the pull of my spirit and committed her time and her hospitality so that I could see beyond my own limited understanding and catch a glimpse of the amazing plans He has for me. I long for the day when I can hug her neck again, yet I feel her in my soul whenever I see a text pop up on my phone or see her beautiful smile on my Facebook feed. And, should the Lord allow, I know that when we visit each other again, the Christ in me will leap at the Christ in her, and I will know that I am bound to her through friendship that transcends distance and even words.

I want to encourage you today to take a risk. To listen to what your heart is telling you when you meet someone new. That woman standing by the wall in the church lobby, she could be your Jonathan—or you could be hers. The one who seems unreachable or you think might be out of your league, she could this very day be begging God to show her a friendship into which she could pour an abundance. The older/younger woman with whom you think you have nothing in common—her story just may be the music your story needs to hear. Be brave, just like Jonathan was brave; he gave up everything and covenanted himself to being in community with David.

God never intended for us to do life alone. He built us to be in relationships with others. We need to cultivate those relationships. We need to see beyond our own desires and plans and be obedient to how the Spirit is leading us. Having friends requires a response of obedience to Christ first and to others second. It requires a humility and a commitment that can often seem scary. But, just know—God has some of the sweetest communion you will ever experience in store when you take the time to answer the call of love, commitment, and covenant with another woman.

CONNECTION QUESTIONS

1. What are some of the themes you see in Scripture verses that reflect the importance of friendship?

2. In what ways has God used your closest friend(s) to show you more of Himself and speak truth into your life?

3. Is there anything you wish your friend(s) knew about you that you haven't yet shared?

CONNECTION CHALLENGE

Do you already have a Jonathan-like friend? Or maybe you've been quietly asking God to show you a woman with whom you can have that special bond? Continue to seek God in prayer, to thank Him for those friendships that already exist, and to ask Him to show you the community He has for you.

However it happens, whether in person or over video chat, spend some time investing in the friendships God has given you.

PRAYER

Dear God: Today I want to pray for my friend _____. I want to thank you for giving me the beautiful gift of our friendship. Help me, Father, recognize the Christ in her the next time I see her or talk to her on the phone. Today while I'm going about my ordinary tasks, may I see her sweet face and be reminded to pray for her and her family. Remind me today, God, that you have designed us to be part of each other's lives and that we are always better together. Bless each of our days, and may we feel the beauty of our friendship even if we're not breathing the same air. Amen.

A Safe Harbor

Create a refuge. A safe harbor. A home with gravitational pull, where those under your roof feel loved and wanted.

"This is my commandment, that you love one another as I have loved you. Greater love has no one than this, that someone lay down his life for his friends. You are my friends if you do what I command you. No longer do I call you servants, for the servant does not know what his master is doing; but I have called you friends, for all that I have heard from my Father I have made known to you. You did not choose me, but I chose you and appointed you that you should go and bear fruit and that your fruit should abide, so that whatever you ask the Father in my name, he may give it to you. These things I command you, so that you will love one another."

JOHN 15:12–17 ESV

ENGAGE

Note three ways you can demonstrate love to your people today simply through the gift of your presence. Simply be with the people God has put in your life.

By Robin Dance

Looking back, I think it was selfish desire that blinded me for so long. I hadn't realized I was anchored to a romanticized version of my past, and that I had allowed rose-colored memory to sow discontent in my present reality. I wanted *what* I wanted *how* I wanted it *when* I wanted, and I was slow to remember that focusing on each tree obscured the forest and its beauty.

In fact, sometimes you get exactly what you had hoped for, longed for, and even prayed for; and yet you still almost miss it because you're looking for an orange when you're handed an apple. Never mind that you prayed for a piece of fruit and that's precisely what you got.

My husband had taken a new job shortly after we married. We were pretty sure it was what the Lord had wanted for us. Sitting on the floor of the Howard Johnson's the night of his interview, we read their Gideon Bible, prayed together, and trusted the Lord with all of our hearts. Certainly it was Him directing our paths straight to this sleepy Southern town.

We decided on a church and jumped in with both feet, joining a just-formed adult Sunday school class, couples in the same stage of life—DINKS. *Remember?* Double-income-no-kids. We studied the Bible in class and out and did a lot of life together. Social outings, weekends away, marriage retreats. We became a close-knit group serving our church, community, and one another. I suppose we were obeying Jesus' command to love one another but, for us, it was simply doing what came naturally.

Then came the baby years. It was more common to hear a "we're expecting" praise on a Sunday morning than not. We celebrated before and after, and for a season our kitchens fed more people outside our families than within.

We tenderly carried those who suffered void and loss. We wrestled together trying to understand how a loving God could allow such pain. Our knees were bruised, fallen in collective prayer, humbled and helpless to do anything but surrender, hope, and trust in Ancient Words and the one who inspired them. It had to be enough because it was all we had.

My husband and I parented on purpose and with careful intention. We prayed. We read books. We sought the counsel of those with children older than ours. We attended parenting classes and conferences. And though we never scripted anything like a family mission statement, I had a personal vision for the kind of home I was trying to shape for our family:

A refuge. A safe harbor. A home with gravitational pull. Where those under our roof felt loved and wanted—our children *and* their friends.

> *A refuge. A safe harbor. A home with gravitational pull. Where those under our roof felt loved and wanted— our children and their friends.*

My dear friend Ashley had described her own home that way during one of our marriage retreats, and it clung to me like second skin. I knew I hadn't felt that way about my own home when I was younger, and I set my compass toward that hope and desire. I never wanted our children or their friends to feel inconvenient to us, though, if I'm honest, sometimes they were. Mostly, any feelings of "mom martyrdom" triggered childhood memories and I'd reorient my thinking to my end-goal:

Our home, a refuge. Gravity (love) drawing them back.

Our families grew, and our love for one another was demonstrated in action. Serving in the nursery quickly gave way to teaching each others' littles in Sunday school. Raising young children can be a blur, can't it? So you might not even notice when your children transition from "learning to read" to "reading to learn."

It was right around that time when my husband accepted a job that would move us, once again, to a city of strangers. I'll never forget the day we told our children, then at the end of kindergarten, second, and fourth grades. We were a puddle of tears huddled in our den, believing this was a trusting-the-Lord, path-making opportunity once again.

Our going-away party reunited our community. I've found Maya Angelo's words so true: *"People will forget what you said, people will forget what you did, but people will never forget how you made them feel."* That afternoon we felt loved and appreciated, as friend after friend shared specific examples of the ways we had impacted their lives. These were word-gifts we might never have known had our moving not prompted their telling.

Treasures piled deep. *Borne fruit.* We praised God for His graciousness and generosity that day, but mostly for the gift of seeing the return on years of investing in people. We might not have been as close as we once were, but we loved this community. We had seen evidence of God's faithfulness and transformative power through *their* lives and that, in turn, ministered to us.

The day came for our family to close that chapter. With all our earthly possessions loaded on a truck, I'll never forget my husband's prophetic words. They would prove to be a haunt over the next ten years:

"When all is said and done, what if we never find community like this again?"

(*Spoiler: We wouldn't.*)

I'm an optimist and a bright-side-seer, and I couldn't even entertain that possibility. Moving to a new place was an adventure! The place we were headed was beautiful, and I embraced it with arms wide open.

I took to heart the wisdom offered by a couple who had moved to our previous hometown right before we left:

"Don't look for a duplicate of the church you're leaving. If you're searching for an exact copy, you'll only find disappointment. Instead, look for a healthy church with sound doctrine. Start fresh and don't try to pick up where you left off."

We knew we found the right church the first week we attended it, though we visited a few more to be sure. Week after week the pastor seemed to be inside our heads and hearts, his messages speaking exactly to our circumstance. It was uncanny. God was so tender in our transition.

Our children assimilated quickly to their new school, faster than we would have dared hope. My husband's job started off well. I volunteered at school as much as I could and joined a community Bible study. We attended an Adult Bible Fellowship with people around our same stage in life.

We did all the things we had always done before to meet people and cultivate relationships. We showed love and exercised the gift of hospitality by inviting people into our home and hosting dinners.

A year passed. *One in middle school now.* Two, three, then four years. *The only year I'll have one each in elementary, middle and high school.* Five more years. *Our first licensed driver!* Six years. *How is my baby a seventh grader?!* Seven years. *How can **he** be driving already? How can **she** be a senior?!!*

Those years passed slowly and quickly simultaneously; time is tricky that way.

And all along community eluded us, no matter how hard we chased it or how much we prayed.

It is interesting and important to note we weren't without friends altogether. But communal depth never took root; we weren't doing life together. We loved "our" people in a general sense, but intimacy was lacking.

We could point to natural barriers:

1. Our children attended a Christian school with a regional draw, making it a challenge to arrange play dates where I might connect with other parents;
2. Our church was also regional, and new friends lived far enough away to make it problematic when trying to make social plans;
3. We lived in a suburban neighborhood, and our house sat so far off the road it was downright hard to be neighborly.

It would be eight years into our move when an eighteen-year-old sitting in my kitchen asked a simple question that caused me to finally see the forest and not just trees—

"Mama D, why do you talk to us? I mean, my mom listens to me and all, but you t a l k with us. You give us so much time. . . ." and her voice trailed in earnest anticipation for my answer.

A light bulb went on.

The veil was lifted, and I was able to see what I had been missing for too many years: I *did* have community! It just hadn't looked like what I had expected.

SOMETIMES COMMUNITY DOESN'T LOOK LIKE WHAT WE EXPECTED.

I proceed to share the story of our newlywed community, and then our subsequent years-long void. While I had heeded the advice from that newcomer to our previous hometown—not to try to duplicate our old church—I had failed to apply the principle to other areas. Instead of being open to a different-looking community, I had tried to recreate the one we left behind.

What I almost missed was the answer to a twenty-year-old prayer:

Our home **had** become a refuge and safe harbor with gravitational pull. There's no doubt our children felt loved and wanted, but that extended to their friends as well. It is no small thing for teenagers to want to spend time with grown-ups, to linger around the dinner table and tell you things they might not have shared with their own parents. To ask questions and to want to hear your answers.

I hadn't been able to gain traction in a peer community, so I had the time and energy to invest in the kids under our roof. Do you see it?

"You did not choose Me but I chose you, and appointed you that you would go and bear fruit, and that your fruit would remain, so that whatever you ask of the Father in My name He may give to you. This I command you, that you love one another" (John 15:16–17 NASB).

It's so clear to me now, I don't know how I could have wrestled against it for so long. In the absence of the community I thought I wanted, I was free to invest in and love on a group of teenagers. They might not have been my first choice for community, but it was never about me anyway, was it? I had the remarkable privilege of God appointing me to bear lasting fruit. Without me even needing to understand, He had invited me to an incredible, holy work; and in the process I had graciously received favor in answer to my prayers.

Our home, a refuge.

CONNECTION QUESTIONS

1. What does it mean to you to learn you are chosen by God?

2. Is there anything in your past that is hindering or subtly undermining your efforts to find community?

3. How does it encourage you to know that God not only chose you but appointed you to bear fruit? What does that look like in your life?

CONNECTION CHALLENGE

Are there people you've been missing while you've been wishing for your community to look a certain way? Invite the Lord to show you what He has for you in the midst of your current circumstance, for your good, His glory, and the benefit of others.

Note three ways you can demonstrate love to your people today simply through the gift of your presence—no fancy meals or elaborate plans. Simply be with the people God has put in your life.

Longing for Loyalty

Loyalty in friendship is an extension of the covenant kindness shown to us by the Lord.

Boaz answered her, "Everything you have done for your mother-in-law since your husband's death has been fully reported to me: how you left your father and mother and the land of your birth, and how you came to a people you didn't previously know. May the Lord reward you for what you have done, and may you receive a full reward from the Lord God of Israel, under whose wings you have come for refuge."

RUTH 2:11–12

ENGAGE

Bless someone you are loyal to with a personal gift (her favorite snack or dessert) to show how much you care.

By Erin Mohring

I t isn't common for a new student to show up with four days left in the school year, so I should have known there was something special about this girl. I wasn't that astute, being a first-grader at the time, but that new student and I eventually became friends, and I thank God for that friendship every day.

Janna and I weren't best friends right away, but we moved in and out of each other's lives based on activities and interests throughout elementary school. Basketball, Girl Scouts, and summer camp come vividly to mind. One summer we rode our bikes all the way across town together for swimming lessons at the outdoor pool, back in a time when cell phones didn't exist. I don't recall ever feeling nervous about that long bike ride, maybe because we didn't think about the evil that could be out there; but I'd like to think it was because we were together. We weren't best friends, but we were there for one another.

As it often goes with girls, we had our highs and lows. Middle school was a time of finding ourselves or just trying not to get lost along the way. We always had our shared love of band, but Janna spent more time at church after finding a relationship with Jesus, and I could be found more and more with the academic team I had joined. We weren't always together, but we knew the other was always there—when one of her long-time friendships fell apart or when I wasn't selected for a certain team. I look back at that time and see ways I could have been a better friend, but I also see growth in both of us that would serve our friendship well in later years. We were still a safe place for one another through the changes of life.

For Janna and me, high school was a time of closer bonding and maturing in our friendship, largely because of shared interests—marching band, service organizations, and similar classes. Friendships take time to develop, and we had more time together in high school than ever. She picked me up for early morning marching band practices, and we could chat about life during that short drive. Weekends were spent rotating between the same four or five homes of close friends. We were a mixed bag of girls and boys of all grades, but I really liked that my friend since elementary school was a part of that group. Familiarity, comfort, and loyalty were already important aspects of friendship for me, and our relationship provided all three.

While there was familiarity, there was also a little something different during our high school years. Janna's relationship with Jesus and involvement in her church were a top priority in her life. Everything she did was impacted by her faith, including our friendship. She was the first one to challenge me about a personal relationship with Jesus. I have to admit this made me quite uncomfortable at the time. As a teenager who had grown up in one faith tradition her entire life, I felt safe and secure in my religious ways. I didn't want to be told I might be missing something, but she was right. She was never pushy or self-righteous about faith, which is why I am confident her questions stuck with me. I was still thinking about them when I gave my life to Jesus the summer after my freshman year of college.

When I read about the relationship between Naomi and Ruth, I see a story of connection strengthened through life changes and trials. Naomi and her family, a husband and two sons, were natives of Bethlehem. A famine in their land forced the family to journey to Moab. In this foreign land, Naomi's husband died and her sons married Moabite women. Within another ten years, both of her sons also died, leaving her with two daughters-in-law, Ruth and Orpah.

Faith was also influential in the story of Naomi and Ruth. It was Naomi's faith in the God of Israel that Ruth saw as something worth following. It didn't have to be that way. Naomi and her family were in Moab, Ruth's territory, and it could have just as easily been Naomi who chose to stick with the local customs and religion. But Naomi's faith was stronger than that, and Ruth took notice. This faith would be life-changing for both of them.

Ruth didn't blindly follow Naomi to Bethlehem when she decided to return to her own hometown. It was a conscious, intentional choice. Orpah, Ruth's other daughter-in-law, did not show the same loyalty, and nobody faulted her for it. After losing her own husband, Orpah initially offered to go with Naomi, but really she wanted to stay where things were familiar. Orpah chose comfort, but loyalty and faith guided Ruth.

But Ruth said, "Do not urge me to leave you or to return from following you. For where you go I will go, and where you lodge I will lodge. Your people shall be my people, and your God my God" (Ruth 1:16 ESV).

These two women endured the death of loved ones, famine, and a long, difficult journey together while still in mourning. The fact that Naomi called herself "Mara," which means bitter, probably means she was not the most joyous person to be around. Naomi's attitude did not deter Ruth, and I'm quite sure she had to grow in maturity to press on in her journey with someone in Naomi's state of mind. And even through Naomi's bitterness, we know Ruth saw glimpses of the older woman's trust and faith in her God.

Hard times are never welcome, but I am mature enough to see the growth that happens in myself when I have no other choice but to cling to God. If I am paying close enough attention, I can also see the help He sends in the form of family and loyal friends.

There were things that could have threatened my friendship with Janna—test scores and boyfriends and college choices—but God was already at work building a deep foundation for our friendship that could withstand any challenges thrown our way.

Janna and I have not lived in the same place since our senior year of high school. We both went to colleges in other states. I stayed in Nebraska, and she moved back home. Texting and Facebook weren't a thing yet, so connecting took a little more time and energy, but we could both tell it was worth it. And we could always meet in our hometown over holidays or school breaks and pick up where we left off without missing a beat. We weren't following one another around physically as Ruth did with Naomi, but somehow our friendship followed us wherever we went and became stronger across the distance.

The greatest reward that came from Ruth's faithfulness would be her place in God's plan of salvation for all of us.

She was one of the first to know when my husband and I got engaged and one of the first we asked to be in our wedding. We went through our first years of teaching together, with very different experiences, but a common understanding and a shoulder to cry on (over the phone) on those bad days. She is the friend who drove miles to see our newborn babies. She was a runner long before I discovered a love for it, but now it is another shared interest. From phone conversations to weekends of my family crashing in her guest room, we are a part of each others' lives as much as any family member.

Loyalty lasts through seasons. It does not bend when lives change and people move and things get hard. Ruth stuck by Naomi when both women lost their husbands. From sorrow to transition to newfound joy neither expected, Ruth was loyal to Naomi, and God rewarded her for it as only He can.

For my dear friend and me, those seasons looked much like the seasons of any young woman—college, life changes, careers, ministry, and moving. Right now we live further away from each other than ever, but our loyalty and connection is at an all-time high.

In Ruth 2:12, Boaz—a relative of Naomi's—says to Ruth, "May the LORD reward you for what you have done." What Ruth did was exhibit unwavering loyalty to Naomi, and Boaz knew that only the Lord could reward her for this extraordinary behavior.

I do not consider my dedication to friends to be anywhere close to that of Ruth, but this story is not about competition. Because of Ruth and Naomi, God has heightened my understanding for intentionally connecting with another believer and the blessings that flow from that relationship. I consider it a reward to have someone in my life encouraging and challenging me in my faith.

This happened for Ruth as well. Ruth grew up in the pagan culture of Moab. It was through her relationship with and loyalty to Naomi that she came to know and love God. We know no greater blessing than the love of God. Ruth's connection to Naomi also led to a new marriage and a child of her own. And from her family tree came the Savior of the world, Jesus Christ. The greatest reward that came from Ruth's faithfulness would be her place in God's plan of salvation for all of us. I stand in awe at the way He works in the seemingly ordinary things of our lives, such as friendship and family, to show His everlasting love.

TRUST GOD. OPEN YOUR HEART. BE THE LOYAL FRIEND YOU'VE ALWAYS WANTED.

Just as I see the hand of God in Ruth's story and my friendship with Janna, I also recognize how difficult it is to form new friendships and develop loyalty as we get older. Not long ago my family and I moved to a new city. I watched as friendships I thought were secure and marked by loyalty fell apart. My own lack of effort definitely contributed to the end of these friendships, but the sting of those losses is still with me. I know I'm not the only woman who has experienced this heartbreak.

Maybe as you read this story, your heart aches because this type of loyalty in friendship has never been a part of your life. That doesn't have to be your story, friend, but it does require three things from you.

1. Trust God. He is the one who put a craving for connection inside of you, and He wants to fill that longing.
2. Open your heart to the friends He brings your way. This is the hardest part, especially if you've been hurt in friendship before. As women enter your life through church, career, school, or other places of community, continue to ask God to reveal the close friends He intends to be a safe place for you.
3. Be the loyal friend you've always wanted. Put your heart out there again by loving others well. I'll be praying God shows Himself faithful in connecting your heart in community with another who shares your love for Him.

We are blessed to be a blessing.

We are not loyal in friendship to receive anything in return. Loyalty in friendship is an extension of the covenant kindness shown to us by the Lord. The only reward we need is knowing God sees and is glorified through our actions. We are blessed to be a blessing.

CONNECTION QUESTIONS

1. Think about a time a friend showed you extraordinary kindness or loyalty. What did that friend do? How did it make you feel?

2. What do you need most from a friend right now?

3. What hurts do you need God to heal so you can move forward in new friendships?

CONNECTION CHALLENGE

Life gets busy with the urgency of home and family and work. Friendships can be unintentionally lost in the bustle, and I desperately want to guard against that ever happening in my life.

Think about friends you connect with regularly, but could connect on a deeper level if fear weren't an obstacle. With that person (or those people) in mind, look for a favorite snack or dessert to make and share. Who could you bless on a more personal level to show that you care and are a loyal person in her life? Show up in her life the way Ruth was present in Naomi's life.

PRAYER

Lord, our hearts long for connection that lasts through the triumphs and trials of life. You have put that longing in each of us, and we humbly ask You to connect us in loyal friendship with others who love You. Help us to follow Your example of faithfulness with the friends You've given us and love others well as You have called us to do. Protect our hearts as we trust Your plan for friendship in our lives. Amen.

The Life You've Been Given

This is your one beautiful life. God has invited you into it to live as YOU, not anyone else.

> "Pay careful attention to your own work, for then you will get the satisfaction of a job well done, and you won't need to compare yourself to anyone else."
>
> GALATIANS 6:4 (NLT)

ENGAGE

Find a way to serve your community with your friends using the skills and gifts you all bring to the table.

By Jennifer Dukes Lee

A new girl showed up at our exercise class last week. I knew her—we'd been in a Bible study together several years earlier—so it was fun to see her walk through the door.

"Yay! You're here!" I said, and gave her a little side hug.

She pulled me aside.

"I'm so nervous, Jennifer. I haven't been in an exercise class for years, and I feel so out of shape," she whispered, scanning the room of athletes.

I put a hand on her shoulder and reassured her, telling her we'd all been there. I told her how the workouts were designed to meet us where we are—no matter our fitness level.

Before our workout began, I quickly shared my own story: One year earlier, I couldn't do more than five burpees in a row without feeling like I was going to lose my lunch. In fact, I didn't even know what a "burpee" was. I thought it was the sound one makes after a satisfying meal. (It turns out that a burpee is a move that is a progressive combination of a jump, a squat, and a push-up.) Power cleans? To me, that wasn't a weight-lifting move. It was what I did to whip my house into shape before guests came over.

She smiled a small smile, the kind that she probably didn't feel on the inside. And then the workout began. That day we were to complete a series of kettle-bell swings, sit-ups, and burpees—each at our own pace.

Within minutes, the new girl was doing what a lot of us do when we're in a room full of other women:

She started to compare.

The only newbie, she had fallen behind the group.

"You're going to lap me!" she said when we were side by side on the mats, doing burpees.

And while she laughed as she spoke, I knew that she was discouraged. I could almost see the energy slipping away.

I prayed a small prayer for her, that she could stay focused on *her* personal best. Our coach has a keychain with the words, "Me vs. Me." In that moment, I gave myself a small pat on the back for living by those words. But my self-congratulatory back-slapping ended abruptly, because about a half-second later, I did something:

I started to compare, too!

I noticed out of the corner of my eye two of our most skilled athletes were doing burpees in graceful synchronization. Like they could seriously star in a CrossFit promotional video.

I felt my own pace slow. My spirits were dampened by a critical self-analysis: "I'm not like them. I'll *never* be like them! After all this time, I should be better than this. I am so ungraceful! I look like a dying fish, flopping on dry ground!"

> "I DIDN'T ASK YOU TO BE HER. I ASKED YOU TO BE YOU."

Right then, God repeated words to me that He has spoken into my heart for the last several years, whenever I start to compare: "I didn't ask you to be her. I asked you to be you."

Maybe someone else needed to hear those words too.

For the last several years, I have traveled around the United States in my ministry as an author and a speaker. (Ironically, one of the main topics I cover is comparison—so it's always a bit humbling when I catch myself comparing, like I did at the gym. Clearly, I am a work in progress.)

During my ministry travels, I have the privilege of meeting many women, and they often share their hearts and insecurities with me. So many of those insecurities are fed by the tendency to compare.

We compare our jean sizes, cleverness, Fitbit steps, marriages, successes, competency, sophistication, ab-flatness, hustle, and more. The means by which we compare ourselves to other women are innumerable.

Maybe you're like me: You don't actually *want* to compare. You don't intend to. It feels so . . . junior high. But comparing ourselves to our friends is so incredibly tempting.

If you find yourself tempted to compare, you need to know this: You are totally normal. Social psychologists even have a theory for it. In 1954, Leon Festinger first introduced the theory of "social comparison."[12] The theory suggests that we determine our worth by figuring out how we stack up against others. The drive within us to compare is very strong. According to Festinger, our desire to compare is a drive nearly as powerful as the drive of thirst or hunger! That's intense.

People have been measuring themselves against one another for approximately forever—sometimes with deadly consequences.

Cain compared himself to Abel, with a jealous anger that ended in his brother's murder (Gen. 4). Joseph's brothers, moved by envy, sold him into slavery (Gen. 37). Jesus' disciples bickered and compared themselves to one another on several occasions (Luke 9).

So if you're tempted to compare, you're not the only one. But even if it's normal behavior, *that doesn't mean it's good for us.*

Paul pointed out the foolishness of it all:

"But in all this comparing and grading and competing, they quite miss the point" (2 Cor. 10:12 MSG).

We might not be killing our sisters or selling them off to the Egyptians. (We do have standards, people.) But are we killing each other's spirits? Are we killing our own souls?

Are we, as the verse says, missing the point? Are we missing Jesus?

I think we are.

It's the kind of behavior that can damage the way we feel about ourselves. But it can also damage our ability to cultivate healthy and lasting friendships with other women. If we are so focused on how we measure up, we'll always find ourselves in one of two positions—feeling better than or worse than someone else. Either way, that kind of comparative analysis is like poison in relationships.

When women compare, two people are hurt—the comparer and the compar-ee.

When we compare, we forget the value of our own lives. We forget that we're the only "us" that the world will ever get.

We forget that God made us *in*comparable.

I'm convinced that comparison is one of the biggest joy-robbers and dream-shredders in a Christian's life.

The Comparison Monster wedges its ugly self smack-dab between us and whatever God is calling us to do: start a blog, write a song, lead a Bible study, apply for a promotion. Nothing will kill a dream faster than looking at the life of someone who's already living your dream, then believing it's too far out of reach for you.

If you can't do it like her, why try?

Can't write like her? Forget it.

Can't make a difference like your friend does? Throw in the towel.

How sad for you, and how sad for the rest of us. You are the only "you" the world gets. We need you to be you in this one life you've been given.

> *We need you to be you in this one life you've been given.*

When we compare, here's what happens:

1. We fix our eyes somewhere other than on Jesus. We are either looking at ourselves or looking at someone else, and we miss the main event—Jesus at work.

2. We will always find someone doing life "better," so we fail to see the good that God created in us. God declared us "very good," but we still discount it as "not good enough."

3. We will perhaps find someone not doing life as well as we are, and we can become bloated in our own self-image. When we do that, we become like the Pharisees, who pridefully compared themselves to other people.

If we're going to compare ourselves to anyone, it better be Jesus.

Comparison creates an us-versus-them mentality that can rob the body of Christ of its unity and fellowship.

Psychologists tell us that when we feel inadequate, we might try to protect our own self-worth by diminishing the work of those we envy.

Psychologist Mary Lamia writes:

> Fearing any eruption of inadequacy or disappointment in yourself can motivate you to protect yourself by diminishing the importance of the envied other by devaluing them. You are engaged in devaluing when you have belittling thoughts about another person, such as petty criticisms. The things you will criticize about those you envy are likely to be qualities that you believe other people admire in them.[13]

When we compare ourselves to others, it's more than a battle we're having on the inside. It spills out of us. Maybe you've seen how it happens. A friend posts on Facebook about the fact that she ran another five miles today, lost another ten pounds, or got a promotion. And when they're not looking, someone might try to knock them down a few notches.

"She's so obsessed with running," someone might whisper about the runner who posts her Nike app route on Facebook.

"I hope she's not neglecting her kids," someone might say with raised eyebrows about the woman who got another promotion.

Two years ago a friend confessed to me that she was so overcome with jealousy toward me that she actually unfriended me on Facebook. At the time, my first book had been published. Meanwhile, she had been working for years on a book idea but hadn't been able to find a publisher. I didn't realize that she had unfriended me until she confessed it, but I had felt an unexplained bitterness from her for all those months. Her comparisons hurt her, and they also hurt me.

My friend Carey told me once how a group of moms had made fun of her for being a "Pinterest mom."

"They talked about how bad Pinterest moms make them feel for not making cute valentines or throwing 'extreme' birthday parties," Carey said. "It was hurtful. I have never in my life gone overboard on my kids' birthday parties in order to make someone else feel bad. I do it because creating special things brings me joy."

We might be tempted to roll our eyes at the precocious comments that some preschool mama quotes. Somewhere inside of us, we might be turning green with envy at another writer's best-selling book, a former colleague's success in a new business venture, another couple's second trip to the beach in a year. We might even quietly harbor a sense of satisfaction when the object of our envy stumbles.

When we see envy rise up, dear Lord, help us tamp it back down.

FRIENDSHIP CANNOT GROW IN THE SOIL OF COMPARISON.

Friendship cannot grow in the soil of comparison.

For the sake of ourselves and our sisters, we must stop this. Life is not a competition. We're actually all on the same team, and it's called the body of Christ.

There's good news. We have everything we need within us to overcome comparison. As Christians, we are given the invaluable gift of the Holy Spirit within us, combined with the authority of the Scriptures that guide us toward right living.

Some important instructions are tucked into a letter that Paul wrote to the Galatians:

"Pay careful attention to your own work . . . and you won't need to compare yourself to anyone else" (Gal. 6:4 NLT).

God has called us each to our own work—in the office, the gym, the home, everywhere. And Paul is telling us that when we keep our eyes on our own work—when we "pay careful attention" to it—we won't need to compare anymore.

If I am focused on my work, I am believing the best about the "me" God created. And I am not making someone else cower under the roaming eyes of my envy.

You know what? We could spend our whole lives wishing for "something different" for our lives, and then turn around to realize that we missed the "something different" we were created to live.

This is your one beautiful life. God has invited you into it. You are not called to live the life of Judy or Katie or Megan. (Unless, of course, you are Judy or Katie or Megan.) You are called to live your life. When I get to heaven, God doesn't want to say to me, "You sure did a swell job of being Crystal!" He wants to say, "I'm so glad you were you, Jennifer."

Furthermore, when we don't compare ourselves, we are giving Judy the space she needs to be Judy, Katie to be Katie, and Megan to be Megan.

Yes, the social psychologists are right. We are going to be tempted to compare. But one of the greatest antidotes to comparison is praise. We can praise God for what He has given us and—this one might be harder—praise God for the unique gifts He has given to our sisters. Instead of envying them, we can rejoice with them. Consider what would happen if we started celebrating other's victories instead of trampling on their parades. What if we begin today by taking God at His Word and living more confidently, knowing He created us uniquely? What if we started living out God's call on our lives, without worrying whether we'll measure up to some invisible standard? And then what if we picked up some pom-poms and cheered on our friends?

When we affirm a friend we are seeing her great value without letting it prescribe something about us.

"Me vs. Me." That's my coach's advice for the gym, but it also applies to our work, our relationships, our weight, our accomplishments, all of it.

I love the way Eugene Peterson paraphrases the verses in Galatians 6:4–5 in *The Message*:

"Make a careful exploration of who you are and the work you have been given, and then sink yourself into that. Don't be impressed with yourself. Don't compare yourself with others. Each of you must take responsibility for doing the creative best you can with your own life."

I was back in the gym the other day, and let me tell you what: my "creative best" was definitely creative. I had my floppy-fish form on display, got tangled in the jump rope, and nearly tripped over my own shoelaces. We were doing a timed workout, and this girl right here came in dead last place.

But you know what?

I got my personal best that day, I felt strong on the inside, and I left the gym with an extra spring in my step—and that was all that mattered.

CONNECTION QUESTIONS

1. Take a few moments to reflect on some of the work God has called *you* to do in the past year.

2. How does it make you feel to know that God trusted you enough to do the job?

3. What is an area of your life where you could benefit by applying the principle of "Me vs. Me"?

CONNECTION CHALLENGE

Praise is an antidote to comparison. This week, go out of your way to affirm a friend who is doing a great job of "doing the creative best" she can with her life. Instead of comparing yourself to her, thank God for how He created both of you for one-of-a-kind purposes.

Prayerfully find a way over time to serve your community together using the skills and gifts you BOTH bring to the table—whether it's volunteering in a food kitchen, donating your talents to teach a class, or organizing a charity run.

PRAYER

Dear Lord, It is tempting for me to get distracted from my own work by comparing it to what everyone else is doing. When I get distracted, whisper into my heart: "I didn't ask you to be her. I asked you to be you." Give me confidence in You alone, knowing I am fearfully and wonderfully made. Keep my eyes fixed on your Son, Jesus, so that I can do what you've called me to do in the kingdom. Amen.

The Hard Work of Friendship

CONSIDER

When we listen more, speak less, and are slow to anger, we build friendships on a foundation of truth and grace.

> "Everyone must be quick to hear, slow to speak, and slow to anger."
>
> JAMES 1:19

ENGAGE

Host some college students, young adult women, or single gals in your home. Not to babysit or help with projects, but simply to pour into their lives.

By Karina Allen

Kat was moving away—but that's not what hurt me so deeply. It was the fact that she didn't seem sad about leaving her family and friends. With quality time as my primary "love language" and us having previously spent a good bit of time together, I'd assumed we would make big plans to do something similar before she left.

We didn't.

Understandably, Kat and her husband spent their final days in town preparing for their move. While I didn't want to take it personally, I did. I wasn't sure how not to feel hurt by what seemed to be her lack of care for our friendship demonstrated in the form of her time. To make matters worse, I fell into my "cold shoulder" default mode instead of reaching out to her. Basically, I was being held hostage by bitterness, resentment, and anger.

Knowing I was in need of godly counsel to help me process, I made plans to have lunch with a mutual friend who is quite a lot like me—a lover of connection, community, and quality time. We prayed through what it could look like to not have my reactions controlled by Kat's behavior. I knew deep in my spirit that her intention was never to hurt me. In fact, I was reminded that I consider Kat to be a beautiful soul who loves and gives and serves well! Just because she and I were dealing with this change differently didn't make one of us right and the other wrong.

After lunch I texted Kat and we had a great conversation. We both apologized for setting unrealistic expectations on the other and for hurting each other's feelings. Instead of piling on guilt we chose to extend grace to one another, which gave us each the freedom to flourish in our own God-given personalities.

Within the unique design God had for each of us, He built three reminders into James 1:19. These instructions apply to each of us, regardless of personality type. In those hard situations, when friendship and community feel the most challenging, James reminds us to be quick to hear, slow to speak, and slow to anger. This sounds great, but how? How do I not react when I've been hurt? How do I pause before speaking in a harsh tone? How do I not speak up in moments I want my voice to be heard?

In the same way that I was able to share my struggle with a friend who was neutral to the hurt I was experiencing in that moment (a "quick to hear, slow to speak" gift I was grateful to receive), sometimes the hard work of friendship requires some godly counsel to help us find our way through. For me, not having strong family ties and being a single woman leads me to rely a great deal on the biblical community around me. For you, those trusted individuals might be your family or spouse, a pastor or mentor. We all have blind spots. Whether financial decisions, relational challenges, or decisions related to calling, take the initiative to reach out to those trusted people around you. These individuals can view those areas with objectivity and spiritual insight while showing what it looks like to be a James 1:19 type of friend.

I've also found that it's important to be that kind of friend for someone else. Instead of gossiping with a friend who comes to me about a hard relationship issue, or becoming angry on her behalf, I can listen, be slow to answer, and share Scripture objectively. When I become a James 1:19 type of friend to those people God has placed in my life, I build relationships that have a foundation of trust and grace. This is true for you too.

It's comforting to realize that the God who created each of us so uniquely is never surprised by any of our struggles. Scripture is full of passages that teach us how to forgive, how to repent, and how to handle challenging relationships. Being human is hard, and being in community can be nearly impossible.

God desires more for us than to just read about what to do when we face conflict. Scripture becomes alive in our hearts when the words move from the page into our minds and turn into action. James 1:19–27 makes the connection between hearing God's Word and doing what it says!

God's intent for His children is for us to live within the context of community . . . authentic, loving, generous, gracious and life-giving community. But this version of community can never exist if we aren't living out the Word of God.

"My dearly loved brothers, understand this: Everyone must be quick to hear, slow to speak, and slow to anger" (James 1:19).

When I first read James 1:19, it almost feels too easy—three simple steps. How hard can that be, right? But when I really think about it, I realize that it's far easier to read than it is to live. To be slow to speak, quick to hear, and slow to become angry all take a great deal of effort on my part. It's a reminder that apart from the Holy Spirit living in me, teaching me to work out my salvation, I'll never be able to be the kind of friend I want to have in my life.

> SCRIPTURE BECOMES ALIVE IN OUR HEARTS
> WHEN THE WORDS MOVE FROM THE PAGE
> INTO OUR MINDS AND TURN INTO ACTION.

I've seen what it looks like in various work environments and communities when we don't live out James 1:19. Small issues turn into larger problems when we're not slow to speak. Miscommunication gives way to arguments when we're not quick to listen. Bitterness and offense run rampant when we're not slow to anger. Assumptions lead to division—the opposite of the unity God desires for us.

Here's the thing—the living and active Word of God is supposed to transform our hearts and bear good fruit through our words and actions. Through the Holy Spirit in us, the Word of God can bring lasting change in how we think, speak, and live.

When we lean on God to work in us and make James 1:19 come alive through our actions, we notice that we can:

1. Extend grace for the "work in progress." We are all in process. We are all in the process of becoming like Christ, conformed to His image. God loves us in the middle of our messes and mistakes, in the middle of pain that others have caused, and He loves us in the middle of a fallen and broken world. We are His beloved daughters. Because we know that God sees the potential inside of each of us, we can extend grace and patience to others and ourselves.

2. Choose compassion. The Bible describes Jesus as being moved with compassion (Matt. 9:36). He not only felt sorrow or sympathy; He went a step further and healed and forgave. He fed the hungry and gave water to the thirsty. Christ cared about both the spiritual and the physical needs of those who were hurting. His compassion compelled Him to act. His action met a need. Because of God's compassion for us, we can ask Him to show us the needs of those around us and choose to offer compassion when community feels challenging.

3. Make room for the Holy Spirit. Although it can be tempting to work in our own power to fix the problems we're facing, God is the only one who can work on our lives from the inside out. When we stand back in grace, peace, and discernment (or when we're quick to listen, slow to speak, and slow to anger), it softens us and allows us to have hearts receptive to correction and accountability. We become a vessel that the Lord can use. We love others with His love and speak His truth, covered in His grace.

4. Invite others into God-designed community. When I read about the early church in the book of Acts, I am blessed, encouraged, and challenged. They did life together in every way possible. They worshiped together, broke bread together, and studied the Scriptures together. They lived the good, the bad, and the not-so-pretty parts of life together. And they continued to pursue community with one another. When we embrace a James 1:19 way of living in community, it can speak volumes to the world around us and gives us the opportunity to invite others to join us to live a life where sisters in Christ genuinely love, care for, and honor each other.

It's been said that God gave us two ears and one mouth so that we can listen twice as much as we speak. May we each learn to listen with our ears, hearts, and minds open. May we believe the best in others, offer them the benefit of the doubt when friendship is hard work, and extend grace as often as possible.

God is constantly calling us to view others through the lens of Christ. It's not always easy or our natural inclination; nevertheless, through the strength of the Holy Spirit it is possible. After all, when God is *quick to hear, slow to speak, and slow to anger,* how could we respond with anything less?

CONNECTION QUESTIONS

1. Think of a time when you were quick to speak and quick to anger with a friend. How did that affect your relationship?

2. Which of the three commands in James 1:19 are most difficult for you: quick to hear, slow to speak, or slow to anger?

3. How have you seen God work in your life when you've been on the receiving end of someone else's compassion and understanding?

CONNECTION CHALLENGE

Relationships are complicated, beautiful, messy, fun, awkward, and delightful. They are all of that and so much more. They are completely worth the time and effort it takes to see them thrive.

Look around your community and your church and make plans to invite a few college students or single gals into your home. Not to babysit or help with any projects, but simply to pour into their lives. Be quick to listen to them and give them a safe place to share their stories. Be slow to speak—loving instead of giving advice.

Why We Need Friends to Carry Us

CONSIDER

Carrying each other's burdens provides a safe space for each other and is encouraging to our souls.

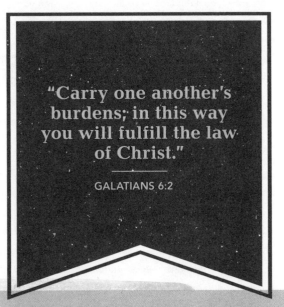

"Carry one another's burdens; in this way you will fulfill the law of Christ."

GALATIANS 6:2

ENGAGE

Take time today to invite a friend to teach you one of her hobbies. As you learn from her, listen to her and help carry her story.

By Bonnie Gray

I didn't know who to call or what to do.

I was crying so hard, I had to pull off to the side of the road. I sat there, feeling disoriented about why I was so upset. Here I was, a forty-something mom of two beautiful boys, happily married to my soul-mate husband. And yet something in me felt so pained, the tears just kept pushing up and through.

Some people have a father wound. It somehow seems easier to talk about that. But I have a wound you don't hear people talk about in Bible studies or share in a circle for prayer requests.

I carry a mother wound. And I'm afraid to confess it. Because I wouldn't want you to judge me or think I haven't forgiven my mother. I have, but while forgiveness is an act of obedience that requires only one person, reconciliation requires two. It's a complicated journey.

Sometimes there are stories we swallow down and keep quiet because we've already suffered a dream lost or love unrequited— and we don't want to risk feeling more alone or rejected by a friend who doesn't understand.

I didn't want anyone to think my family was broken. I didn't want anyone to think *I* was broken.

So I did what we often do. *I kept quiet.*

But sometimes it takes more faith to accept the truth—in order to find the courage with Jesus to let go of trying to fix things we were never meant to carry alone.

Maybe, like me, there was no one you could trust with your heart completely. You've had to make a way for yourself in this world. But deep inside, even though you hide, *you crave to be known.*

This quiet burden of staying silent with our stories comes with a cost. Maya Angelou says it this way: "There is no greater agony than bearing an untold story inside you."

God understands this craving to be known. He whispers to us, "Carry one another's burdens" (Gal. 6:2).

I needed what God desires for each of us to experience: a friend to help us carry the burden of an unfinished story.

Are you or someone you know in the middle of an unfinished story? *Is God inviting you to find a friend to carry the burden with you? Or is God inviting you to help carry the burden with one of your friends?*

Then we have to take the risk. To invite someone in.

Although I understood the importance of letting others in, taking steps to do it hasn't been easy. I didn't want to jeopardize how people viewed me, both among friends who seemingly had wonderful, loving family relationships and among ministry in the church community.

Until one day I started experiencing increasing feelings of anxiety. I started worrying so much about any and every little decision. I'd lie restless at night, desperately praying for God to release my exhausted self to sleep. I felt sad, trapped, and overwhelmed by emotions I'd always been able to control.

It seemed the words my mom said to me, whether it was a phone call or a stressful conversation, left a continual cloud over my mind and heart.

To cope, I doubled up on my Bible reading and prayer. I did whatever it took to set my mind on the goodness of God. Listened to praise music. Read all the books on putting the past behind me. You name it, I did it.

But this is the thing: everything I tried, I did alone.

Until the day I had to pull over because I couldn't see through the tears. This was the day I had to face the reality of my circumstances and what I really needed in order to walk through this season. It was time to be honest with myself.

I feel hopeless. The thought scared me and left me shaken.

I was learning what we all eventually come to learn: *We weren't created to journey alone. We need each other.*

In that moment of confusion and fear, someone's face popped in my head. When I was leading ministry at church, Carol was a mentor for me in an advisor support role. The last thing I wanted Carol to know about me was that I was feeling hopeless.

She might ask me to step down from ministry. She might tell the entire pastoral staff about my problems. I quickly pushed the notion out of mind. I couldn't risk it.

But one day Carol invited me out for lunch at a deli by the shoreline.

It was there, as I watched the soft glimmer of the sun sparkle on the water, I felt something I hadn't felt in a very long time.

I didn't want to be alone anymore.

The burden was too heavy to bear. I began to tell her my story. Before I could finish, I started crying.

I expected Carol to say all the things I feared, but my world changed in one instant.

Her eyes softened and she said, "Well, if I had a mom like that, I'd feel pretty hopeless too." And for some reason, it made us both laugh. Then I stopped to cry some more.

She listened. She didn't try to fix me. Instead of giving me advice or quoting Bible verses, she did something that changed the shape of my heart.

She helped me carry this burden by sharing parts of her unfinished story with me instead.

She became my friend.

Carol's ability to love me is an example of how Christ, through His Spirit, empowers us to bear one another's burdens. As a matter of fact, Christ Himself knows exactly how it feels to be overwhelmed with sorrow and how to share those deep emotions. In the Garden of Gethsemane, Jesus said to His three closest friends:

> "My soul is overwhelmed with sorrow to the point of death. Stay here and keep watch with me." (Matt. 26:38 NIV)

Jesus was honest and transparent letting them know what he felt. We can only presume to know His reasons. Maybe He needed support? Maybe He was helping to prepare them for His unfinished story? What we do know is that He shared and asked them to stay awake. Then He went a little further away to pray to the Father:

> Jesus fell to the ground . . . "Father . . . Please if it's possible, take this cup of suffering away from me." (Luke 22:41–42 NLT)

What a picture of agonizing these verses display! He was not only honest with His most trusted friends, but He pleaded with the Father more deeply and intimately than is possible with another person.

Jesus did what none of us could do. He willingly took the cup and bore the burden of all our broken stories alone on the cross. He did that so you and I won't have to suffer the same fate.

Jesus gave us each other. We don't have to journey alone. He gives us the ability to carry each other's burdens.

There are parts of our story that can't be told with a beginning, middle, and end. We are all walking on a journey with Jesus through an unfinished part of our story.

We are all in the middle of something.

We weren't made to suffer through this unfinished journey alone. We were made to be in community. In the same way God spoke the first light into the darkness with His voice, God gave each of us voice that was created to be heard. To be known. To be understood.

God has made a way to meet this need—through you and me.

If you're craving to find a friend who can carry the burden with you, here are three tips that have helped me find that friend:

1. **Don't wait. Initiate.** Jesus spent a lot of time with His disciples before some closer friendships developed, eating, walking, and relaxing together. Find someone compatible with your style of sharing. Enjoy a low-key, casual hangout time together.

2. **Be curious. Ask about their stories.** Questions are gold. I've found that if I ask someone to share their stories and they are comfortable being transparent about their feelings, it's a good indication they would be comfortable hearing mine. Test the waters a bit. Be curious about the other person and their stories. Give them the gift of listening.

3. **Give your friend permission to just listen.** Well-meaning friends often give advice because they may not know how else to help. Letting a friend know we just need her to listen frees her to be present with us. I say something like this: "I want to tell you about _____ . I don't need advice, but I really need someone to just listen and know what I'm going through. Is that okay with you?"

If you feel prompted to be that friend to someone, here are ways my friend Carol helped me carry the burden:

1. **Give the gift of your time.** We often make time to meet to do ministry work or study Scripture in Bible Study. These are important, but to carry each other's burdens your friend needs to connect with your soul. She needs space to experience friendship with you. Make time to share something you enjoy and invite her to join you. In that space, she may come to trust that you care deeply about her as a person and truly desire to know her.

2. **Give the gift of listening.** Ask your friend questions that give her the opportunity to share. Be inquisitive about how she sees a particular situation. Rather than asking questions to troubleshoot your friend's problems or to give advice, give her permission to be known. Heard. Understood. Listening allows your friend to unburden her heart. The Holy Spirit can use that listening space to comfort your friend and refresh her heart as she discovers what God may be prompting her to receive or experience.

3. **Give the gift of your unfinished story.** When you share how you experience similar feelings or struggles (circumstances may be different), you bring comfort and encouragement to your friend as a kindred spirit rather than putting more pressure on her to perform or be perfect. Christ empowers you to do for her what He does for you—identify with the moments of weaknesses and struggles. You free your friend from feelings of inadequacy, guilt, or shame. The apostle Paul shares, "To the weak I became weak" (1 Cor. 9:22).

There are so many stories still taking shape in each of us. It's the beauty of what it means to be living letters of Christ.

Our stories are still being written. Carrying each other's burden by providing a safe space for each other gives our souls strength to keep picking up our pen. To write with faith.

It's not always easy. But sometimes the harder stories are the ones worth telling.

CONNECTION QUESTIONS

1. How is God prompting you to share your unfinished story?

2. How can you let Jesus heal a hurtful memory by being present with you, loving you with His total understanding, reliving it with you again?

3. How can you help carry the burden for a friend?

Dear Jesus, there's a quiet burden I've been carrying that has been so heavy. I don't want to bear it alone. Give me courage to believe it doesn't have to be this way anymore. You see the craving in my heart to be known. Give me courage to let someone in. Prepare the way for me. Send me a friend I can confide in. Give me wisdom to know who that might be. Help me experience a new way of living. Amen.

CONNECTION CHALLENGE

We need friends for this journey of the soul, and sometimes the best way we can create a safe space for those stories to be shared is by investing in the lives of our friends.

Take time today to invite a friend to teach you one of her hobbies. As you learn from her, listen to her and help carry her story. Spending time together opens the door to deeper connections with one another and opportunities to encourage one another to grow deeper with God.

Spur Her On

CONSIDER

Spur one another on toward love, courage, goodness, and a God who is intimately in love with us all.

"Iron sharpens iron, and one man sharpens another."

PROVERBS 27:17

ENGAGE

Host a book club! Invite some ladies to your house or a nearby coffee shop, and explore some new books (or introduce them to your current favorites).

With my mother deep in the midst of her chemotherapy treatments. strength seemed, to me, as nothing but an illusion. I was not feeling strong—I was feeling desperately untethered to anyone or anything. The earth appeared to be shaking, feeling as if it would crumble around me at any moment. Jesus, on the other hand, was consistently steady as I thought I was going to split apart.

It was during this season a few years ago that God placed a girl named Sarah smack into my precarious and shaky life. She was sharpening me before I realized I was being sharpened. This, I am learning, is what it looks like to be human. We feel pain and joy and raw, ruthless grief. We hurt and love and shatter, and then we get sewn back together. But most of all, we need one another. Deeply. We need one another more deeply than any of us can possibly say.

Each day I wake up and long to be loved as I am. There are many times when that happens and many times when it doesn't. There are days when, instead of waiting for a person to love me for me, I trade in my waiting for a false sense of belonging. I convince myself other things will fill my void, but I'm always disappointed.

In reality, the only one who loves me unconditionally is Jesus. I've just recently succumbed to the wooing of His love, finally surrendering. (Surrender is not my strong suit.) He is a good, good God, and when I unfurled my clenched fists, I began to see His love in ways I never had before.

Liv, Kath, and Sarah are some of the clearest and most tangible ways God has shown His love to me.

Liv, my older sister, is the caretaker, nurturer, and one who looks out for me—as well as everyone else. She is my logic, my practicality, my voice of reason, and my best friend in this whole wide world. (God knew I needed someone to say, "Aliza, if you do that I will actually get on a plane right now and come find you," when I suggested I was going to hitchhike in Rwanda. At the time it seemed like a great idea to me, but she quickly put an end to that.)

Kath, my sister's longest and oldest friend and therefore mine too, is the compassionate world traveler who helped me fall in love with the world, but mainly with our first love, Africa.

And Sarah is my dear pal and built-in therapist. I could almost get overwhelmed with how much these three believe in me.

If our lives were like tree stumps—with rings and rings and rings around us—these three girls would make up one of my closest rings. We celebrate the good things together, and we mourn the sad, the hard, the lonely. We sharpen each other as kindly as we can. We trade roles: sometimes the sharpener, sometimes the sharpened. Occasionally we hurt one another, because we are all humans and consequently are utterly imperfect, but the basis of our friendship is love. And the foundation of our love is Jesus.

In Hebrews 10:24 (NIV) it says, "And let us consider how we may spur one another on toward love and good deeds."

Who are you spurring on toward love? Who is spurring on you? Who are you sharpening—with vulnerability, and kindness, and grace? Who is sharpening you? They may not always be the same person.

My girls in my inner rings spur me on—toward love, toward courage, toward goodness, and most importantly, toward a God who is intimately in love with us all. It's a fantastic cycle. Because they spur me on, I can spur on others.

In order to have that cycle of spurring—as well as the kind of friendship that sharpens one another—you must begin with vulnerability. One of my favorite quotes about vulnerability comes from Brené Brown. In her book *Daring Greatly*, she says, "Vulnerability sounds like truth and feels like courage. Truth and courage aren't always easy, but they're never weakness."[14]

The only way those inner rings can work fluidly is if you start with vulnerability. I remember when Sarah and I hardly knew each other. We were sitting in her car around midnight, and she turned to me and said, "Aliza, how are you doing?" It was in the midst of my mother's chemotherapy, and for a long time I had felt like I couldn't breathe.

When I started to tell her how I was feeling, the words didn't come. (A rare occurrence for me.) Instead of words, a tidal wave erupted from inside my chest, and suddenly I was crying all over her. Let me tell you—I am not a pretty crier.

As I got out of her car, I contemplated how crazy she must've thought I was. I figured surely our friendship was toast. Why would she want to hang out with me again after I sobbed all over her?

And then she texted me: *I'm praying for you. I'm so glad you were able to talk to me tonight. You're brave. Any time you need to talk again, I'm right here.*

That sealed our friendship for me. Not only did Sarah encourage me to be vulnerable, she cultivated a safe environment in which I could do so. I had prayed for a long time that God would put someone in my life who I could honestly connect with. To my delight, surprise, and fear, He plopped Sarah right in the midst of it all. It's perpetually terrifying to be vulnerable with someone. But the depth of friendship produced from vulnerability is a beautiful, tender gift.

The depth of friendship produced from vulnerability is a beautiful, tender gift.

And then there's accountability. Who doesn't love to be held accountable? I'll raise my hand to that. I have enough pride to say that accountability is not my favorite thing in the world. It's not exactly comfortable when someone says, "Aliza, I'm not so sure if how you're acting lines up with what Jesus thinks."

Accountability is not an excuse for blaming or judging someone. Accountability is kind and is dependent on three things:

1. Active listening: "My dear brothers and sisters, take note of this: Everyone should be *quick to listen*, slow to speak and slow to become angry." (James 1:19 NIV, emphasis mine)

2. A non-judgmental attitude: "*Do not judge*, or you too will be judged. For in the same way you judge others, you will be judged, and with the measure you use, it will be measured to you." (Matt. 7:1–2 NIV, emphasis mine)

3. Caring for one another: "And he has given us this command: Anyone who loves God *must also love their brother and sister.*" (1 John 4:21 NIV, emphasis mine)

I'll take my wounded pride and—hopefully—their words within my heart, reviewing both my actions and their opinion on the matter. If I set aside my ego and let go of any offense I might feel, I'll soon realize that my friend is not only showing me love, but sharpening me in the process.

"As iron sharpens iron, so a friend sharpens a friend," Proverbs 27:17 (NLT) says wisely. We know vulnerability and accountability are key for a sharpening friendship, but there's one more ingredient I might be tempted to add: authenticity.

FOR VULNERABILITY AND ACCOUNTABILITY TO EVEN BE POSSIBLE, WE MUST ARRIVE WREATHED IN AUTHENTICITY.

For vulnerability and accountability to even be possible, we must arrive wreathed in authenticity. The definition of *authentic* is not false or copied, genuine, real.

In a world where we're bombarded by advertisements that promote layering ourselves with masks and facades, authenticity is hard to find. We can compare ourselves to the people we see in the media, or we can become hurt by words we read online. But sharpening the way God designed is not meant to be literally sharp or hurtful. It is meant to be kind. A friendship where both people enter genuine and true, shedding their layers at the door, opening up with one another as who they are—instead of who they think they should be—is absolute authenticity.

You see, God meets us exactly where we are. No matter the circumstance, God is meeting you here, in the precise place where your feet currently stand. He doesn't ask us to become a better person in order to meet with Him. He doesn't demand perfection or holiness before we open our mouths to pray. He simply asks us to be authentic and real with our Lord—to rip off the masks the world suggests we keep and instead rest in who He created us to be.

Resting in who we are sounds so much more refreshing than struggling to maintain a mask of perfection, or a facade of having it all together.

God designed these sharpening kinds of friendships so they run deep, and wide, and deeper still. The shallow waters are not where we become sharpened. Safety is not where we grow. Only when we take risks—when we're vulnerable, authentic, and held accountable—can we realize how much more freeing it is in the deep. Only when we dive can we understand what we'd be missing if we stayed on the shore.

My sister's husband takes this spurring and sharpening to an entirely new level. He has taught me more about what being a disciple of Jesus looks like than anyone I know. One day each week he meets up with two or three of his friends who don't yet know God. He'll buy them dinner and take them out to a movie, or they'll play a board game or two. He is, quite simply, a kind friend to them. He does not try and coerce them into going to church with him, or convert them into a relationship with Jesus. Of course he doesn't hide his love for God, and he often tells them about Him. But these friends are not his project, and he is not their savior.

I think investing in others, at the same time we are being sharpened by our friends, is the most important part.

Sharpening is a continual, lifelong process. If we wait until we're "fully sharpened" to go out into the world, well, we'll be waiting quite a while. Spurring one another on does not end with our friends who are devoted followers of Jesus. If sharpening and spurring ended with that, we'd be missing the whole point of the Great Commission.

"Go and make disciples of all nations," Jesus said in Matthew 28:19 (NIV). God does not leave us alone to do this. He does not expect us to dig into ourselves to find the strength to tell others about Him. Instead, He provides us with people who will love and sharpen and spur us on, so that we are able to go out and make disciples of all nations.

It is far too easy to stay in our safe and comfortable bubble of Christianity. I speak for myself when I say this. I'll admit to you: it's scary to tell someone about Jesus. It goes right back to vulnerability. But people are not our project, and we are not their savior. Instead, we can look at how Jesus did things—He was kind, He was relational, and He was a friend. That's how we should do things, too.

As we go out into this world, there are a few things we can focus on.

First, if you don't have a friend whom you can sharpen, or who sharpens you (remember, they may not be the same person), I encourage you to ask God for one. God delights in giving us good gifts!

Second, choose one or two or three people in your life who you commit to discipling. Focus on them just as they are, not as whom you think they should be. Love them well. Serve them. And maybe buy them some dinner or play a board game or two.

As people, we have been hurt and loved and shattered and sewn back together. We have the capacity to do this and more to others. Whom will you love? Whom will you sharpen? Who will you spur on to go out into this world? And then, who will do all of that for you?

CONNECTION QUESTIONS

1. Which of these three areas do you struggle with most—vulnerability, authenticity, or accountability? Which comes easiest for you?

2. What has Proverbs 27:17 meant to you in the past? How has the meaning changed for you over the course of different friendships and experiences?

3. How can you help sharpen a friend today?

CONNECTION CHALLENGE

Being the type of friends who sharpen one another means spending intentional time together. Gather on a regular basis and encourage one another. Hold each other accountable. Be vulnerable. Be authentic. And then spur one another on to each corner of the world.

Host a book club! Invite some women to your house, or a nearby coffee shop, and explore new books (or introduce them to some of your current favorites).

PRAYER

Jesus, You are a good God. Thank You for Your promises to us, how You love us and care for us and provide for all of our needs. Please provide the kind of friends who will sharpen us kindly and spur us on—and may we be that for someone too. Please give us the courage to be vulnerable, authentic, and understand accountability. May we be women who sharpen kindly, instead of causing pain. May we love people for who they are, and not as we think they should be. Thank You for accepting us just as we are. We love You.

Your Story Might Be Someone Else's Life Preserver

CONSIDER

True friendship can feed you and sustain you through the hardest of seasons.

"Rejoice with those who rejoice; weep with those who weep. Be in agreement with one another. Do not be proud; instead, associate with the humble. Do not be wise in your own estimation."

ROMANS 12:15–16

ENGAGE

Share your story first so that someone else might feel comfortable opening up about theirs.

I was sixteen and growing up in South Africa. And up until my junior year of high school, my biggest worry had been trying to figure out how to grow my bangs out with some semblance of cool and getting the boy on the swim team who drove the sweet motorcycle to notice me.

One night after youth group, however, I stepped off the edge of a cliff and into a black hole of adult worry for which no one can prepare you. It was a typical Friday night. We were all hanging out at the familiar house that was home to our church's youth group and finishing up some praise songs and probably an entire tray of pizza.

I was surrounded by friends who'd known me since first grade, and we were all fascinated by this work of growing into the teenaged versions of ourselves. The girls figuring out new ways to style our hair, and the boys flirting with the girls over cups of steaming hot tea and their guitars. This space—the people, the house, the games—was ordinary and beautifully safe. This space felt like home to me. This space could be trusted with games of Uno and a faith that felt as comfortable and familiar as my favorite pair of black boots.

But when I glanced over into the side study I noticed my father in tears. There are moments when you know, even as you're living them, that you've just passed a monumental mile marker in your life. Moments that you will look back on for decades because those were the moments you remember feeling the earth shift unexpectedly.

My dad was crying, and one of my best friend's father was trying to talk to him—comfort him, I guess. I looked away because it was so foreign and so weird to see my father crying, but I couldn't stop the knot I felt creep into my stomach and wrap itself around my insides. So by the time my little brother and I got into the car and my dad started driving, the air was thick with the dread of anticipation. We sat and waited, and I'm sure there was a part of me that didn't want him to start talking.

But he did. As we headed up streets as familiar to me as my name, my father spoke words I didn't recognize. He described the sickness that had been creeping through my mom's tired body for months without any of us realizing it. When you're sixteen, or any age for that matter, the word "cancer" brings a conscious consideration of the possibility of death.

One minute, you consider yourself all grown up and then in the next second you can find yourself trying to climb into your dad's lap like you did when you were a baby. And he'll have to pull over into an empty parking lot because his children have reverted to the toddler versions of themselves as snot and tears run down their faces and they try to wipe them on his shoulder.

That was the night I was born as an adult. There was nothing cool about it. Grown-up news will force you to grow up. And it will be nothing like the music videos promise.

Sharing news like disease and the potential of death with your friends forces you all into a new dynamic. Conversations that used to start with concerts or music or radio stations and favorite DJs morphed into discussions about cancer and the effects of morphine on your mom's weird hallucinations. And right there in the hallway between your English class and your science lab you discovered who your friends were. Because they were the ones who still found a way to make you laugh.

We laughed as much that year as I cried. We laughed at the things that teenagers find funny, and then we spent as many afternoons talking about the things that were no longer PG. Life and death became as interchangeable a conversation as hair and makeup. My friends went there with me. There into the darkest nooks and crannies from which the young are usually sheltered. There through the opened doors that none of us had visited before. There into hard rooms where we sat in the uncomfortable spaces and silences because that is the kind of conversation that cancer invites. Whether you want to come in or not. It's there waiting for you on the other side of the door. And as the daughter of a dying mother

I was forced to walk through it. My friends could choose whether or not they wanted to follow.

They did. They came. They came on Saturday afternoons, swinging by the house in the old yellow Mini Cooper one of us finally had a license to drive. They'd pick me up and tell my dad they were taking me out for coffee. And I'd sit in the car sandwiched between friendships that never expected me to make small talk. Friendship that didn't expect me to unpack all the heavy baggage that was following me around. Friendship that was just content to let me sit in silence and absorb all their easygoing life.

That kind of friendship gets under your skin and revives your soul. That kind of friendship already knows all the things you don't have the energy to say out loud. That kind of friendship lets you sit at the table while everyone orders cappuccinos and maybe a plate of fries to share and lets you breathe in the normal of everyone else's lives.

I lived on that feast of friendship for the eighteen months between my mom's diagnosis and her death. That friendship was manna to me. I couldn't have described what made it so special when I was living it, but looking back I understand better now.

I understand that the most profound gift we can give one another is being willing to simply sit with each other in our darkest moments. No explanation required. No pep talks or halfhearted promises about how it will all turn out well. Instead, being willing to sit in the uncomfortable truths with a person, agreeing their right now is terrible, helps the person survive their right now. I survived on the generous gift of the presence of my friends.

They just kept right on showing up. Whether I returned their calls or not. Whether I was in a good mood or not. Whether I snapped or laughed or cried, they didn't once, in eighteen months, stop showing up. Romans 12:15 tells us to "Rejoice with those who rejoice; weep with those who weep." I was the beneficiary of the life-changing, radical impact of those words the year I turned seventeen. They changed me. They saved me. The friends who threw themselves as living life pre-servers into the dark and terrifying sea of grief simply by offering to share my sadness helped me not to sink. I held onto them even on the days when it looked like all I was doing was sipping a latte in a coffee shop.

I was white knuckling, hanging on by my finger-nails to the people who were willing to weep with me over diagnoses that kept going downhill. And to those who would rejoice in days of late afternoon sunshine and new driver's licenses. And others who would spend evenings listening to the latest mixed tape someone had compiled.

The best kind of comfort sometimes shows up in disguise as that friend who isn't bothered by your silence.

Comfort doesn't have to look like a sermon or a wordy card or an awkward conversation. The best kind of comfort sometimes shows up in disguise as that friend who isn't bothered by your silence. And simply folds themselves onto the sofa with you and watches the game and passes the popcorn. If we want to comfort those around us who are aching and breaking apart, we don't need to over think it. Most days we just need to be willing to show up.

And the showing up can make us feel awkward. It might make us feel embarrassed. But only for the few minutes it takes us to stop thinking about ourselves. As soon as we're able to look past ourselves and focus on our heartbroken friend, our beloved family member, our desperate child or neighbor or coworker, the sooner we're able to forget about saying the right thing and simply start saying the next thing; we'll forget about ourselves.

You might be surprised how helpful that is to keep in mind. Just say the next thing—pepperoni or cheese? Coffee or tea? Here, I knitted this for you. No need to return the pie dish. I picked up coloring books for the kids. Where's the laundry so I can fold it while we watch a movie together? Just keep showing up and saying the next thing, and that kind of friendship will wrap itself around the hurt simply by your willingness to be present.

My friends kept showing up as my mom slowly disappeared out of her skin over the course of eighteen slow months. Each day was a testimony to how:

Friendship will feed you even on the days you don't think you can possibly get out of bed.

Friendship will sustain you and somehow, completely unexpectedly, friendship will still stumble onto joy in the very middle of the worst bits.

There were days we laughed so hard—like that time we tried to dye our own hair without running it by our parents. The shock and surprise at hair dye that should have been red but left a whole head of hair nearly black. And gracious parents who laughed with us and leaned in and taught us how to choose the right color and how to work from the roots of the hair down to the tips. There were afternoons of hot dog sandwiches and late nights listening to John Cougar Mellencamp out by the pool. There was always tea and always space for silence right in the middle of the group. The story of cancer didn't eat me alive. Instead, I learned how to keep living right through the very scariest parts—how to hold onto being alive because my friends were so full of life and so willing to share their stories with me on the days I didn't know how mine would end.

It's humbling to receive that kind of friendship. I imagine it's humbling to offer it as well. It takes such a deep gift of vulnerability to be willing to let each other into the parts of us that ache as well as the parts of us that are spilling over with delight. We wrote each other into a shared story that junior and senior year of high school that I can still close my eyes and step back into two decades later. Take it from this forty-something mom who remembers much more vividly than she would like what it felt like to live the story of losing her mom at eighteen—everything you pour into that person next to you or in your church or in your book club whose life is imploding is going to last them a long, long time. And it will give them a new story.

I know how to hold tight to the hands next to me. I know how to offer my own hand. I know how to show up and I know how to cry and I know how to make space for laughter even on the bleakest days.

If you know that too, then your people need that gift from you. If you've ached and broken and had people put you back together simply from their refusal to quit showing up, then you know how to do that now. And your people, the ones in your living room, around your dining room table, at your back door, hanging out in your college dorm, they need that from you now. They need you to share the story of how we don't have to walk through the worst bits of life alone. They need you to do the hard, deliberate work of showing up and saying the next thing. So that they remember they are not alone.

CONNECTION QUESTIONS

1. What hard things have you lived that will help you connect more deeply with the people around you?

2. Who can you think of that desperately needs to know they're not alone in what they're going through right now?

3. How is God asking you to show up for someone today?

CONNECTION CHALLENGE

Having been on both the receiving end and giving end of "showing up," I know that neither position is easy. Friendship is hard work. Spend some time in prayer, asking the Lord to give you the courage and discernment to share your story with someone.

Hearing your story of struggle could be just what someone who is walking through a dark valley right now needs. Let them know that however they're feeling is okay with you. That you're a safe place to let all their feelings out. Good or bad. Share your story first so that someone else might feel comfortable opening up about theirs.

PRAYER

Dear Jesus, thank You that nothing about our stories scares You off. Nothing shocks You. No valley is too deep or too dark for You to find us, hold onto us, and pull us through. Help us to be Your hands holding tight to the people around us who feel like their lives are breaking into tiny pieces. Hold tight to all that brokenness through our hands and our stories. Make us brave, so that we keep showing up, no matter how awkward it might feel, and keep sharing our own stories as we help our people live through theirs.

Faith is taking the first step even when you can't see the whole staircase.

– MARTIN LUTHER KING JR.

CONNECTING

WITH

(COMMUNITY)

MORE

INTENTIONALLY

We're Stronger Together

Community means we win together and lose together. We cheer each other on, hold each other up, and keep Jesus at the center of it all.

"A cord of three strands is not quickly broken."

ECCLESIASTES 4:12 (NIV)

ENGAGE

Practice going from "me" to "three" and connect with two people this week.

My friends and I sat cross-legged on a flower-covered comforter. There might have been a pop star poster gracing the bedroom wall. Certainly we had enough hairspray on our bangs to qualify our little group as a fire hazard. We giggled about boys as we braided colored threads and slipped them onto each other's wrists. When school started in a few weeks we would have a visual declaration that said, "Someone likes me. Someone chose me. Someone wants to share life (and a lunch table) with me." In other words, I have *people*.

Friendship bracelets first became popular in the 1970s and they continue to be summer camp favorites. For many of us, these bracelets may be our only experience with creating something that could be called a "cord" or "rope" in Scripture. Historically, braided ropes weren't for decoration or adornment; they served important practical purposes. So when Solomon said, "A cord of three strands is not quickly broken" (Eccl. 4:12 NIV), his listeners would have instantly understood the depth of what he meant. But for us that short phrase could use a little more explanation.

For example, the number of strands mentioned in this verse is significant. According to the *Cambridge Bible for Schools and Colleges*, "'Three was for the Israelites the typical number for completeness, probably because the rope of three strands was the strongest cord in use."[15] As believers today, we also recognize that "three" is the number of the Trinity: Father, Son, and Holy Spirit. And we often hear this verse used at weddings to talk about the strength of two people plus Jesus.

While there are certainly divine illustrations to be found in Ecclesiastes 4:12, there's also a lot of insight for how we live in community. The pattern of "three" in relationship appears to be significant in our human connections. A recent study showed that the average person has "2.03 confidantes." A "confidante" was defined as someone the responder "had discussed 'important matters' with over the previous six months."[16] In other words, the most common social system in today's world is made up of three people. (A side note: In a world where it seems everyone has tons of friends, we can take comfort in knowing that if we even have a couple of folks we connect with in a meaningful way, then we're doing just fine.)

Psychological research also supports the significance of "three" when it comes to relationships. The Bowen Center says, "A triangle is a three-person relationship system. It is considered the building block or 'molecule' of larger emotional systems because a triangle is the smallest stable relationship system. A two-person system is unstable because it tolerates little tension before involving a third person. A triangle can contain much more tension without involving another person because the tension can shift around three relationships."[17]

One person is an individual. Two people make a relationship. But when we get to "three" we have *community*. We have become something we could not be on our own. The strands are now a strong cord.

In our busy world the question naturally becomes, "Why bother coming together?" We've been taught to look out for number one, to pull ourselves up by our own bootstraps, and that we can be anything we want to be . . . all by ourselves. And relationships are messy. They're complicated. At times they're downright painful. It seems like the risk could outweigh the reward.

To answer that question and those concerns, we need to look closer at the purpose of a "rope" (we'll use that word since it's more common in our culture and is a synonym for "cord").

First, a rope is created to help withstand tension. Most of us are familiar with the game tug-of-war. A group grabs each end of the rope and then pulls with all their might. Whoever drags their opponent across a line in the middle wins. But the participant that always seems to get the worst of it is the rope itself. It has to deal with demands from both sides. It gets stretched in opposing directions. It has constant stress. Does that sound like anyone else's life besides mine?

Our world is like a big game of tug-of-war. The needs of our families pull on us. Then a work deadline comes, and we have to stretch in that direction. We look for relief at church and instead sometimes feel like we're given a list of expectations that yank us into guilt. How can we survive all this? We need other "strands" to help us bear the weight. Ecclesiastes 4:12 says, "A cord of three strands *is not quickly broken.*" In other words, *without community we snap.* We've all had those moments when we've had enough and we simply lose it. We say things we don't mean, we make choices we're not proud of, we fray when we really want to stay and be strong.

We need to be able to send a text that says "having a bad day—please pray." Maybe meet with a friend (or two) over coffee and get gut-honest about the struggle we're facing. Even invite a few people over for dinner and let the laundry wait while we remember what it's like to laugh. *We can't take the tension of life all by ourselves.* We need to share it with others or we'll be pulled to pieces.

> WE CAN'T TAKE THE TENSION OF LIFE ALL
> BY OURSELVES. *WE NEED TO SHARE IT WITH*
> *OTHERS OR WE'LL BE PULLED TO PIECES.*

Also, a rope is created to help with heavy lifting. Think of a pulley system. Individual strands would not be able to withstand the weight placed on them, but together they become a powerful force that can be strategically leveraged. There are a lot of burdens in this world. Every day we encounter needs. All around us are hurting people. Our good intentions often lead us to believe we need to solve every problem for every person. But God never intended for us to live this way. We're part of the body of Christ. It's only as we come together with other believers that we can truly be effective. We're not called to do it all; we are called to do our part. When we try to bear the weight of the world by ourselves we're going beyond being servant hearted—we're trying to be Jesus. And we are also asking for burnout. Eventually something within us will give way and we simply won't be able to continue.

I've lived this reality. For years I thought that "ministry" meant singlehandedly meeting every need that came my way. I often lived outside the gifts God created me to offer, ignored who He created me to be, and neglected my own health and well-being. When depression and anxiety threatened to consume me, I sought help from a counselor. She helped me see that the expectations I had for myself far exceeded the expectations God had for me. I needed to surround myself with others whose strengths complemented my weaknesses, who could share the load, and who would be energized by what drained me. As I relinquished what God never asked me to do in the first place, I found a renewed sense of passion, joy, and purpose. I was doing *less* but making a difference *more*. That's the power of coming together.

Finally, a rope is created to help with security. I've become a bit obsessed with superhero shows and movies the last few months. I like the battle between good and evil (especially since in these scenarios good always wins). A theme I've noticed is that bad guys are always getting tied up. To trees. To chairs. To the nearest non-moving object around. The heroes of the story understand this: you can't let your enemy run wild and free if you want to win the battle.

We'd be wise to remember that as well. Whether we realize it or not, we have enemies too. We fight the negative thoughts in our mind. We combat the enemy of our souls who would love to see us fall. We must defeat discouragement, doubt, and fear. If a superhero tied up a villain with a single string, we'd expect mayhem to ensue. But when we try to deal with our opponents on our own we're doing the same. We gain strength when we join together with others who will speak truth to us on the days we can't remember it, who will pray fiercely on our behalf, who will help hold back all that threatens us. When we *come* together we can *overcome* whatever we may face.

Even when we understand the purpose of community we may be confused about the process of it. How do we begin connecting with each other? Or if we already have bonds with others how do we become closer?

Before a rope can ever be formed, the strands must be prepared. In ancient times that meant natural fibers would be smoothed so that they were ready to join with others. For us I believe this means first taking a close look at our hearts. We can ask God, "What's in my heart or life that might interfere with community?"

Here are a few common ways we can make our relationships rougher than they need to be:

Pride. It's easy to look at others and think, "I don't need you," or even, "I'm better than you." Those thoughts keep us from intertwining our lives. Humility says, "I'm not created to do life on my own," and "Even if you're different than me, you have something to offer."

Insecurity—We may have the opposite of the thoughts above (I tend to). We think, "No one needs me," or "Everyone else is better than me." Those statements are just as effective at keeping us away from others. Instead we can say, "God has given me a place in the body of Christ and good gifts to share."

Unforgiveness—Nothing frays our souls like unforgiveness, bitterness, and resentment. They're like barbs that cut those around us. Before we can become braided into the rope, it helps tremendously to start the process of healing. I say *start* because forgiveness is an ongoing work in our lives. We only need to be willing to say, "Lord, please help me learn to forgive."

Thankfully, our struggles don't disqualify us from community. Our hearts will never be fully "smooth" in this life. A strand doesn't need to be perfect; it simply needs to continue letting the rope maker work on it as needed. And it's often in community that more of those rough places get smoothed out.

The next step in the process is braiding. For us, that means coming to a place where we're willing to share our lives with others. The strands in a rope aren't parallel; they are interconnected. Andrea Mitchell says, "I firmly believe Satan doesn't want us to have community with others, especially other believers. It's extremely hard for someone to steal your joy or redirect your focus when you are surrounded by like-minded people. Rather, when we isolate ourselves we start to listen to the lies that fill our mind that no one else would ever allow themselves to get to this rotten point, that we are a failure, a loser, with no hope. He knows that when we hide ourselves away in the dark, we are more apt to invite him in."[18]

True connections take time, commitment, and courage. While social media can make it seem like bonding is as easy as clicking a "like" button, we're called to go deeper with each other. And that means making relationships a priority. Our season of life and circumstances will impact our capacity for connection, but we can all pause and ask, "What can I do to truly connect with the people I love?" Even a little bit of time or encouragement can make a big difference.

Being intertwined also means choosing to stay even when it's hard. We live in a fallen world, and we are fallen people. That means inevitably conflicts will come, personalities will clash, and disappointments will happen. The most obvious choice is to withdraw and protect ourselves. And in cases like abuse or other patterns of destructive behavior, that is also the wisest. But often we leave to avoid the messy process of loving one another. We think there must be a better friend, group, or church out there and abandon the people right in front of us in search of "better." But the reality is just as we will never be perfect, we will never find a perfect community. In this world there are only in-progress people (including us).

We become stronger when we learn to stay because the strands of rope depend on each other. What happens to one happens to all of them. We're told, "Rejoice with those who rejoice; weep with those who weep" (Rom. 12:15). We're to share the happy and the hard of life. Sometimes we plaster on a smile and pretend that we're okay when we're dying inside. Other times we hold back because we fear the jealousy or resentment of those around us. But community means we win together and lose together. We cheer each other on, hold each other up, and keep Jesus at the center of it all.

But community means we win together and lose together. We cheer each other on, hold each other up, and keep Jesus at the center of it all.

That kind of community is possible because the ties that bind us together aren't simply human. The friendship bracelets I made years ago inevitably fell apart. But Colossians 1:17 says, "By Him all things hold together." We can have hope for our relationships because Jesus is in them. Will there be difficulties? Yes. Will we have conflicts? Yes. Will we walk through seasons of loneliness? Yes. But do we have to do life alone? No.

Somewhere inside me there's still a girl sitting cross-legged on a flower-covered comforter. And with all her heart she still wants to be able to say, "Someone likes me. Someone chose me. Someone wants to share life (and a lunch table) with me." In other words, "I have *people*." That desire never goes away because it's placed there by God. We may try to ignore it or shut it up, but it will keep coming back. We are not made to be individual strands. We are meant to be part of a strong cord. One that can't quickly be broken. One that can bear life's weight. One that connects us to the God who created us for each other.

CONNECTION QUESTIONS

1. What kind of friend do you want to be for others?

2. What scares you most about connecting? What is a truth from Scripture that can help you overcome that fear?

3. How has God been a faithful friend to you?

CONNECTION CHALLENGE

As you consider the community God has placed in your life, pray that God will work to smooth edges and create friendships equipped to do the heavy lifting of life—together.

On a piece of paper, list who God has placed in your life. Then practice going from "me" to "three" by connecting with two people on your list this week.

To take it a step further, why not grab some thread and make friendship bracelets together to wear and remind you of God's love for you, for your friends, and for your community.

Gifts of Value

God has created you, exactly how you are, for a unique purpose. Only you can fill the role He's designed for you.

"So the eye cannot say to the hand, 'I don't need you!' Or again, the head can't say to the feet, 'I don't need you!' But even more, those parts of the body that seem to be weaker are necessary. And those parts of the body that we think to be less honorable, we clothe these with greater honor, and our unpresentable parts have a better presentation. But our presentable parts have no need of clothing. Instead, God has put the body together, giving greater honor to the less honorable, so that there would be no division in the body, but that the members would have the same concern for each other. So if one member suffers, all the members suffer with it; if one member is honored, all the members rejoice with it."

1 CORINTHIANS 12:21–26

ENGAGE

Take a spiritual gifts assessment and create a list of ways you can use your gifts to serve your community.

When I first joined the staff at my church, I was encouraged to serve in different ministry areas to get a feel for what we do, gain an understanding, and see if maybe a new area of service might be right for me.

It wasn't a bad idea, but I'm not sure it worked as intended. I was already leading a small group and volunteering in the children's department, but since I wanted to be a team player (and, you know, not get in trouble at my new job), I signed up for the Sunday morning hospitality team.

On the surface it seemed like a good fit. Reasoning that I sometimes enjoy baking and trying new recipes, whenever I take one of those spiritual gift assessments, and hospitality always shows up in my top five on those spiritual gifts assessments.

So I volunteered to bring snacks a couple times a month. And while I think I made some kind of muffins that first week and some no-bake cookies another week, I quickly resorted to stopping at the grocery store for boxes of cookies or even—at my lowest point—bags of tiny donuts.

I was so embarrassed. Week after week I would slink into the kitchen, hoping to avoid seeing anyone as I added my sad (or so I thought), store-bought baked goods to the snack supply. Week after week I would feel guilty for not having time or making time to mix up something delicious at home, for not contributing something more from-scratch than from-store.

Eventually I became so ashamed of my apparent lack of hospitality that I stopped volunteering. I explained to my manager and the woman in charge of Sunday snacks that I needed to focus on the other areas in which I was serving. They were kind and understanding, possibly because they'd seen just how uninspired my service was.

What an opportunity I missed! Between my insecurity over my ability to do what I thought was required and my not-so-subtle judgment of hospitality as a less-than gifting, I lost out on the chance to serve my community as well as the chance to be part of a smaller team serving together each Sunday morning. I presumed to know what God intended, what I was made for, what the church needed—and I missed the simple joy of living out my part of the body.

In the years since that misguided attempt to serve on the hospitality team, I've realized a few other things.

First, it did not matter ONE SINGLE BIT that I brought snacks I hadn't made from scratch in my own kitchen. Having a daughter who insists on visiting that snack table between services each week, I now realize that it really is a matter of quantity not quality when the kids descend on that table! And as a "mean mom" who instructs her child to choose just two items, NONE OF WHICH should be a cupcake with loads of frosting, I have a whole new appreciation for those flat, from-the-store cookies.

It turns out that I was the only one judging my store-bought snacks. The rest of the hospitality team was simply glad to have something to put on plates before the next wave of hungry kids (and their parents) arrived.

Second, even though I do enjoy having people in my home and planning parties (hence the high score in hospitality), that's not actually the gift God was using during those months.

Paul provided three separate lists of spiritual gifts in his letters (found in Romans, Ephesians, and 1 Corinthians). The lists include different gifts, so it's possible that they are simply examples of the ways God gifts His people rather than a comprehensive guide to the only ways one might serve the Lord. With that in mind I realized, well after my pride led me to quit serving in the hospitality department, that my experience with Sunday morning snacks wasn't about my ability to gather a group of people together for fellowship over a meal. No, it was about my tendency toward responsibility.

I love personality tests. But when I took the test that said one of my top strengths is responsibility, I was so disappointed. Responsibility? How dull! How boring! I mean, it is fitting for this spreadsheet-loving, list-making girl whose top spiritual gift is administration. *But why*, I wondered, *can't I ever get something a little more exciting?*

In case you're wondering, I'm not sure what gift or skill or strength would feel exciting or glamorous or fun enough. Perhaps one that leads to travel and stages and pedicures on a regular basis? Or maybe one that makes me super popular—liked by all the most likeable people. The fancy gifts, you know? The ones that the cool people have, the ones that everyone notices and appreciates, the ones that result in fabulous parties and widely read articles and— let's just throw this in—great hair?

Yes, those are the gifts I want.

But those—whatever they are, if they even exist at all—are not the gifts I've received. My strengths and spiritual gifts are more practical, and they include responsibility—meaning that even when I didn't have time to bake, I could be relied on to provide something (anything!) for people to munch on before and after church.

While I thought my packaged snacks were a pitiful offering, something to be ashamed of, something to sneak into the kitchen before anyone saw the plastic boxes and bags, bringing them was actually an act of obedience and a way to live out the responsibility that I feel so strongly, that God gave me. The hospitality team didn't need someone to create amazing baked goods; they simply needed someone to show up with some food.

And show up I did. I served God and others with a strength He gave me, even though I didn't understand it at the time. Honestly, I still sometimes struggle to appreciate the value of that strength.

My short stint in the Sunday snacks department was not the first time I'd misunderstood or undervalued the talents God has given me. I remember two instances very specifically.

First, when I was in college, I was involved in a campus ministry. As soon as I was eligible (read: a mature, wise sophomore), I applied for a position on the leadership team. I wasn't sure which area of ministry would be the best fit for me, but I sure didn't think it would be the Tech Team.

Making promotional videos? Designing a website? Running the sound equipment? Boring! Who wants to do that? Not me. I just knew that when the campus pastor looked at the list of open positions and compared it to the list of interested students, my name was merely the last one unmatched and, therefore, the logical fit for the stupid Tech Team (as I so maturely called this ministry team I served on that year).

Then, several years later, my husband and I joined ten of our closest friends in planting a new church. We decided to start our church with in-home meetings about the different areas of ministry on which our church would be founded, and each couple was assigned an area to lead. My husband and I were assigned to the Fellowship Ministry.

Fellowship. As in potlucks and picnics. Again, I was disappointed because clearly this wasn't the best place for me to serve God. Obviously, I fumed, I could be doing so much more than planning chili cook-offs!

In both cases I'd signed up to serve God with expectations I would get to do it in fun, splashy, impressive ways of my choosing. Who wants to update a clunky, late-90s website when others get to plan spiritual retreats and help people find small groups or mentors? And discussing and planning social events seems much less important than missions or discipleship or anything other than fellowship!

But God—unsurprisingly—knew what He was doing, in my heart and with my ministry. The year I spent on the Tech Team in college? It prepared me for a little hobby called blogging and the jobs I've held (and loved) in social media. And leading our church plant's Fellowship Ministry? That taught me about community and friendship and the real meaning of fellowship—and gave me loads of inspiration for my e-book about planning parties.

THE GIFTS AND ROLES THAT WE SEE AS LESS-THAN
ARE OFTEN THE ONES THE LORD VALUES MOST.

Those jobs—just like my gifts—weren't any less amazing just because I judged them less special than others. They were the exact roles God needed me to fill—with the exact gifts He's given me. And just because I deemed fellowship "less spiritual" than other ministries and responsibility as "less fun" than other gifts doesn't mean that God sees them that way.

As a matter of fact, the gifts and roles that we see as less-than are often the ones the Lord values most. First Corinthians explains that well:

> In fact, some parts of the body that seem weakest and least important are actually the most necessary. And the parts we regard as less honorable are those we clothe with the greatest care. So we carefully protect those parts that should not be seen, while the more honorable parts do not require this special care. So God has put the body together such that extra honor and care are given to those parts that have less dignity. This makes for harmony among the members, so that all the members care for each other. (1 Cor. 12:22–25 NLT)

The Greek word for fellowship, *koinonia*, isn't the only thing I learned during my time as a church planter. It does, however, illustrate this idea beautifully. Koinonia is a complex word that roughly translates to our concepts of community, sharing, and joint participation—which is not too far from the beautiful way God created His Church to be a body of many parts with equal importance.

God truly did take a box full of unique puzzle pieces of people and move us until we clicked together to make one picture.

I saw this in full force during that season of starting a new church with a group of friends and fellow believers. Even during the times when stress and uncertainty caused our differences to build friction between us, I couldn't help but feel awe as I looked at the way our different personalities and skills and experiences and gifts fit together so beautifully. God truly did take a box full of unique puzzle pieces of people and move us until we clicked together to make one picture.

Maybe you're like me and you've resisted or even resented the gifts God has given you. Perhaps you've wondered why you aren't more musical or eloquent or crafty, why you aren't better at praying or healing or speaking truth to the masses. If that's you, if that's your struggle, I encourage you to stop looking at any gift as better than another. Remember that God has created you, exactly how you are, for a unique purpose. Only you can fill the role He's designed for you, with your specific gifts and strengths, no matter how exciting they may or may not seem.

We shouldn't doubt the value of the gifts God has given us for one more minute. As Paul wrote to the church in Corinth, all of the parts of the body are important.

> The eye can never say to the hand, "I don't need you."
> The head can't say to the feet, "I don't need you." (1 Cor.
> 12:21 NLT)

Your gift—no matter how big or small it seems to you—is so important. We need you! We—the Church, the body, your community—need the you that is unique and valuable and crucial to finishing our puzzle. We need your faith and your prayer and your service and your preaching and your guitar-playing and your muffin-making. We need your leadership and responsibility and motivational speaking and encouraging writing and compassionate listening. We need exactly what God has given you, and you need what He's given me, too.

No matter how God uses my gifts moving forward, I'm determined to stay focused on the Truth that each gift, each part of the Body is honorable. And as I see my sisters and their gifts used by Him and honored, I will rejoice and be glad, because He is a great, creative God who calls each of us to play our part for His purpose.

CONNECTION QUESTIONS

1. How do you think taking a spiritual gifts assessment might change how you serve in the future?

2. Have you ever found yourself wishing for someone else's gifts or believing that some gifts are more desirable or more impressive than others? How do you combat spiritual gift envy?

3. Think of a time when you tried to serve or minister in a way that did not come naturally. Now think of a time when you were serving in your "sweet spot," using the gifts God has given you to serve and minister. What were the differences you felt during each experience?

CONNECTION CHALLENGE

If you haven't taken a spiritual gifts assessment, take one now. You can find several tests online. Once you have your results, read through them carefully and write down ways you've seen these gifts utilized in your work, at your church, in your neighborhood, or at a ministry in your city. The Lord has not only uniquely gifted you; He's also placed you in very specific places.

Take the next step to see how the Lord will continue to use you in your community. Volunteer at church or at a local sporting event or theatre, invite your child's teammates and families to your house for a cookout, or begin after-school tutoring with a child who is in desperate need of help.

PRAYER

God, you are so creative, and I thank You for the way You have taken care with every detail of my personality. I thank You for the way You weave together those who follow You, using our gifts and strengths in ways we might never have imagined for ourselves. Please reveal to me the ways I can use my gifts to serve You, and help me pursue Your purpose for me with gratitude and grace. Help me celebrate the way You've created my sisters in Christ, and show me how to embrace my role in Your Church as we work together. Amen.

Cultivating Creative Community

CONSIDER

God connects us in beautiful and powerful ways with people who share our passions.

"Now we ask you, brothers and sisters, to acknowledge those who work hard among you, who care for you in the Lord and who admonish you. Hold them in the highest regard in love because of their work. Live in peace with each other."

1 THESSALONIANS 5:12–13 (NIV)

ENGAGE

Sincerely acknowledge the work of someone who inspires you to seek God in creative ways.

By Jennifer Ueckert

I have always loved art. Any kind of art. All kinds of art. It was my favorite class in grade school, and I always wished for more of it. I could not wait to get into high school where I could actually take a couple of creative classes. We didn't have many, but I took everything that was offered. I came to find out many of my fellow students did not share my same desire to learn about and create art. For most of them, the art classes were the "easy classes"—a class where you didn't have to do too much or work too hard for a good grade. It was a bit disappointing to my creative heart.

But then it was time for college. My decision to attend an art college wasn't a difficult one. Art in every classroom. Art in the hallways. Carry art supplies to school instead of books. Finally. These are my people. I found my people. A school full of creatives. To finally be surrounded by people with the same heart for creativity as me was such an eye-opening experience. A true gift from God to be around people who just "got it." Who got me. I was simply overjoyed.

Years passed—I graduated from college, married into military life, etc.—and while staying as creative as I could, I no longer had a creative community around me. We moved a few times before we settled into a wonderful country life near a small town. This quiet little spot in the country was not exactly a hub of artistic activity— beautiful, but not what my creative heart longed to experience. I was determined to find people who shared a similar passion for and love of art.

I took online art classes and joined a few online art groups. And I began to share my life online—my love of art plus my love and gratitude for the One that put art into my life. As a girl after God's heart, I wanted my life to point right back to Him. Once I did that, everything changed. I found my people. I found people who loved Jesus and were not afraid to show it. People who shined His light in amazing and creative and beautiful ways. People who understood having paint on half of your clothes and paint brushes around every sink. People who had just as many paint splattered mugs as they did non-paint splattered mugs. Best of all, people who thanked God with so much gratitude for their messy, creative lives. The connection found in those moments was real.

I learned that we must allow ourselves to be seen. It takes courage to step out and share our passions and heart with others. There are so many people who feel that very same way. They are trying the same things and enjoying the same passions. We can feel alone in our work, but I am here to tell you that we are not alone. Courageously stepping out provides moments of authenticity where we experience true connection with others that can develop into real friendship.

From these larger groups and many online connections, I began to grow deeper, more meaningful friendships. Being in a season of not having artsy friends living near me, I have found community, love, and encouragement from my creative online friends. Relationships like these don't come into our lives by accident. God has blessed me with the most creative, compassionate, generous, passionate, and gifted people. These women are not in my life by chance. God is always at work. He connects us in powerful and beautiful ways. He provides exactly who we need in every season of our lives. He has chosen these priceless women so I can see the depths of His love right here and right now.

Online friendships can be seen as lacking real connection, but I think that is so far from the truth. God can absolutely span distances. God can absolutely align hearts. God can absolutely meet our needs right where we are in real life. He fills the desire for connection in amazing ways. He intentionally places us in community where we can grow in ways we cannot grow on our own. A community where we can find encouragement, support, and loving involvement. He builds us up in incredible ways. We just need to open ourselves and open our hearts to it.

I hear God through my online community. He encourages me through them, loves me through them, teaches me through them. He opens my eyes to the beauty around me through them. That is real. He uses them in such amazing ways. I learn so much from watching these women live out His truths. They bring me hope. They give me courage. They inspire me to reach. I see how they are brave, and that encourages me to step out and be brave. God's love is poured out through each of us and into our art, and we stand together to serve Him with our gifts.

God intentionally places us in community where we can grow in ways we cannot grow on our own.

Of course things are not always perfect in this online artsy community. You find competition and comparison, others not wanting to share, and jealousy. Sad, but true. When one is self-focused, serving is lost. But there is no competition in serving God with our gifts. In true, God-honoring friendships, you don't need to compete—we are meant to serve.

- You don't push people down, you lift them up.
- You don't hurt, you encourage.
- You don't criticize, you honor.
- You don't withhold, you share.

We each have our own unique abilities and talents, but we all have the same goal. We have the same calling:

- We all want to put beauty and encouragement into the world.
- We all want to reflect God's love and inspire others.
- We want all glory to be given to Him.

My friends continually point me toward greater faithfulness in the life He has given me right here, right now. Real life. There is no competing in that. It is not about who contributes what or who contributes more or who might be better known. We don't have to worry about all that. They teach me to be open to discovering all my talents and gifts and using them. We discover and we share. No one is worried about the spotlight. There is no "better" than, no "more" than—just following our purpose. Following the passion He put in our heart and sharing in a way so that others would seek Him. All for Him. All for His glory. All of it pointing to Him.

All for Him. All for His glory. All of it pointing to Him.

It is amazing to watch friends grow and spread their creative wings. We get to stand alongside them and cheer them on and root for one another. Cheer as they reach goals and support and encourage when things don't go as hoped. They inspire me endlessly. We can be passionate together without the worry of competing, like I've found in some areas of the art world. When I see joy bursting from a friend covered in paint or clay, it overwhelms my heart. When I see a friend breathe a sigh of relief after completing her last class edit, it overwhelms my heart. Because we speak the same language, and I get it.

Just as God wants us to succeed, our real friends truly want us to succeed. Just as God believes in us, our real friends truly believe in us. They are right there to root us on when we need it. They know we will be right there cheering them on when they need it as well. There is peace knowing a friendship like that, a friendship of loving like Jesus and not competing. A peace that fills our hearts because He pours out love without measure.

This is my creative journey. This is my life journey. These are my people for the journey. We are in this together. We share life at a distance. Even across the miles, it is amazing how tightly He can bring us together. They accept me, encourage me, support me, and love me. They hold me up, dream with me, cheer me on, and challenge me. We are at our best when we are walking together on this journey.

We share our process and learn from one another. We talk about the same internal battles and gain strength from knowing we are not alone. They receive my words with compassion and understanding. We celebrate the same victories, both large or small and praise Him in it all. We stand together, rejoicing and celebrating in the triumphs. We stand together, holding one another up and praying in the struggles. They remind me to see beauty when I have forgotten. They remind me Who this is all for when I have forgotten.

WE ARE AT OUR BEST WHEN WE ARE WALKING TOGETHER ON THIS JOURNEY.

They are seen. They are known. They are loved. They are celebrated. By God, and by me. Part of having deep friendships is being a really good friend. Sometimes we encourage, and sometimes we are the ones encouraged. I want to be a reflection of God's love to others. I give because that is the kind of friendship I hope to receive.

These relationships require time and effort and truth. You can begin by expressing your gratitude often.

Acknowledge one another in specific ways. Tell them how much you appreciate their help and support. There is always something to be thankful for—do not be afraid to tell them! Cherish them, build them up, love them well, and pray for them.

Let these beautiful women change your life. You can experience the most miraculous work of God's hand in your life through these relationships. Be real. Love deeply. He uses these relationships to grow us closer to one another and closer to Him. The Lord will use you.

My friends have taught me so many important things. I love their art, but I love their hearts even more. They have opened my eyes to new ways of seeing and creating. They have taught me not only about my creative path, but also about life. This is friendship. His gift to us. For these connections, my life has been forever changed, and I am overwhelmingly grateful.

CONNECTION QUESTIONS

1. 1 Thessalonians 5:12–13 encourages us to hold others in the highest regard in love because of their work. How can that help us to become the friend we wish we had?

2. If you find yourself competing for the spotlight, how can you focus on encouragement, rather than competition?

3. How has recognizing your God-given creativity drawn you closer to God?

CONNECTION CHALLENGE

Do you know someone who creatively shares God's love or His Word? Maybe their photos capture the beauty He has created around us. Maybe they make Scripture images to share on social media. Maybe their paintings point right to Christ.

Take some time to sincerely acknowledge their work. Tell them how beautifully their work lifts you up. Tell them how they reflect God's love. Tell them how their work is bringing glory to Him. Encourage them to keep sharing for His kingdom while you share their work with your community.

Wildly Influential

CONSIDER

Be the one to initiate connection with old friends or grow relationships with new friends.

"So many people gathered together that there was no more room, not even in the doorway, and He was speaking the message to them. Then they came to Him bringing a paralytic, carried by four men. Since they were not able to bring him to Jesus because of the crowd, they removed the roof above where He was. And when they had broken through, they lowered the mat on which the paralytic was lying. Seeing their faith, Jesus told the paralytic, 'Son, your sins are forgiven.'"

MARK 2:2–5

ENGAGE

Plan a Girl's Night Out—a movie night, a "make and take" event, or a favorite things party.

I am wildly influential among my friends," I joke to my husband. Laughing about it is my defense mechanism, and this is the line I use when I invite a group of girlfriends over and the turnout is small. The numbers are more noticeable since I tend to over-invite. I'm the girl who doesn't want to hurt anyone's feelings and, let's face it, as the mother of eight children, I embraced a the-more-the-merrier attitude a long time ago. With the help of the fancy stationery on my computer's e-mail program, I compose beautifully formatted invitations accented with coordinating photos, almost Pinterest-worthy. Still, I rarely gather a crowd. We live off the beaten path so it takes an extra effort to visit us: a scenic drive past open fields and old barns, where cows leisurely chew the cud and swish their tails as you pass.

I found comfort in that excuse—our remote location—until recently, when my daughter filled our house with wall-to-wall teenagers at her sixteenth birthday party, summoned with nothing more than a text message. Clearly *someone* in our house is wildly influential among her friends.

And yet . . . I've discovered the women who find their way to my front door are precisely the ones who need to be here, the ones I most need to connect with, and the ones who most need to connect with me. If you crave friendship, you're more willing to drive that extra mile or rearrange your schedule to make it happen. When (in)courage sponsored a worldwide day of local meet-ups called (in)RL (in real life), I hosted them in our home for three consecutive years. The attendees ranged from old friends to women who arrived on my doorstep, knees knocking, not knowing a soul. It takes a deep longing for connection to draw a woman from the security of her home and compel her to take a chance at friendship with women she's never met. One new friend drove over an hour to be here.

And recently, I hosted a "Make and Take" party where four of us gathered in my kitchen to create an assortment of health and beauty products enhanced with my beloved essential oils. In my usual fashion, I invited thirty-three women. Did I mope about our final numbers? Heavens, no—I was too busy making sugar scrub! When I overheard my old friend tell my new friend, "Whenever Dawn invites you over here—come! The food and the parties are always like this!" I positively glowed. Each time I pulled out a new recipe for another homemade product—we made stress away bath salts; all-purpose household cleaner; a coconut and olive oil-based, lavender-infused healing salve; sugar scrub; and little glass perfume bottles filled with uplifting fragrance blends and topped with roll-on applicators—they squealed with delight. We were junior chemists pouring Epsom salts, counting drops of oil, diluting cleaning solution, melting beeswax pellets, and measuring granulated sugar. All evening, my old friend exclaimed, "This is your best party ever!" and "This is my favorite thing we've ever done!"

As personally gratifying as a kitchen overflowing with women might have been, I wouldn't trade the memory of that intimate gathering for a steaming mug of Earl Grey on a wintry day, and that says a lot.

It's evident from reading the gospels that although Jesus often found Himself surrounded by crowds, He preferred the company of an intimate few: His disciples and closest followers. We might call Jesus the original small group leader. He came to reveal the mystery of the wisdom of God to man, and in so doing He offered Himself to God as the ultimate propitiation (atoning sacrifice) for our sins, and to us as both Savior and friend. Because of Christ's dual nature as both God and man, we not only know him as king—"King of kings, and Lord of lords" (1 Tim. 6:15 NIV)—but also find comfort in the knowledge that He considers us friends: "Henceforth I call you not servants; for the servant knoweth not what his lord doeth: but I have called you friends; for all things that I have heard of my Father I have made known unto you" (John 15:15 KJV).

It's difficult to wrap our brains around the fact that Jesus Christ is both fully God and fully man, but Scripture tells us that it is so. While we worship Him in His deity, we cling to Him in His humanity. His divine nature gives Him the power to hear and to help us, but His human nature—thirty-three years of day-to-day living here on Earth—enables Him to truly understand us. When you cry out to Jesus in prayer, He intimately understands your needs: "For we have not an high priest which cannot be touched with the feeling of our infirmities; but was in all points tempted like as we are, yet without sin" (Heb. 4:15 KJV).

> WHEN YOU CRY OUT TO JESUS IN PRAYER, HE INTIMATELY UNDERSTANDS YOUR NEEDS.

Mark 2:2–5 tells the story of a dense crowd that so completely surrounds Jesus He can't be easily reached, and of four faithful followers who take extraordinary measures—literally raising the roof—to enter into His presence on behalf of a sick friend. They possess a desire for connection with Jesus so great that we still talk about it two thousand years later.

> So many people gathered together that there was no more room, not even in the doorway, and He was speaking the message to them. Then they came to Him bringing a paralytic, carried by four men. Since they were not able to bring him to Jesus because of the crowd, they removed the roof above where He was.

And when they had broken through, they lowered the mat on which the paralytic was lying. Seeing their faith, Jesus told the paralytic, "Son, your sins are forgiven." (Mark 2:2–5)

I love the way these verses in Mark end: Jesus heals the sick man by forgiving his sins in that intersection where the friends' faith and Jesus' mercy meet. What a powerful testimony! But even as the story convicts me, it also shames me. Do my actions display that level of trust? So often I turn to Jesus—and even my friends—as my last resort. Do I understand that He loves me? Can I trust my friends with my problems? Although the answer is yes, I have to do more than understand: *I have to believe.*

I am ridiculously self-reliant. Maybe the sick man was too. I wonder if he asked his friends to take him to Jesus or if they decided for him. It took tremendous effort to reach Jesus, but they were willing, not for themselves but for their friend. Will you fight harder on a friend's behalf than your own? Although I recognize my dependence on God and my need for the fellowship and support of my friends, I tend to believe that no one has time for me; that my problems are insignificant; that I should keep to myself and avoid getting hurt. Sometimes I even embrace the lie that I don't really matter to Him or to them. I'm willing to bet you do it too.

Do you believe that Jesus can fulfill your every need? That what you say and feel matters to Him? That He sticks closer than a brother (Prov. 18:24)? That He truly cares? That He is mighty in your defense? You are never, ever invisible to Him. When you doubt—when you need a reminder of His love for you—remember these verses and His promises:

- "But the very hairs of your head are all numbered" (Matt. 10:30 KJV). Jesus is aware of every sparrow that falls from the sky, and He values you more. He knows the number of hairs on your head.
- "Look at the birds of the sky: They don't sow or reap or gather into barns, yet your heavenly Father feeds them. Aren't you worth more than they? Can any of you add a single cubit to his height by worrying? And why do you worry about clothes? Learn how the wildflowers of the field grow: they don't labor or spin thread. Yet I tell you that not even Solomon in all his splendor was adorned like one of these!" (Matt. 6:26–29). The Lord attends to the needs of the birds of the sky and lilies of the field, and you are much more important to Him than they are.
- "No one has greater love than this, that someone would lay down his life for his friends" (John 15:13). Jesus loves you so much that He gave His *life* for you, the ultimate sacrifice.

We are the temple of God, the habitation of His Holy Spirit. When we serve one another in friendship and love, we do His work here on earth as the hands and feet of Jesus. His message was radical two thousand years ago: Defend the weak; love the poor; it is better to serve than be served; put the needs of others before your own. When we love our friends sacrificially, we do the radical work of Jesus today. We change the world.

When we love our friends sacrificially, we do the radical work of Jesus today. We change the world

God wired us with a natural desire for friendship more powerful than our introversion, self-reliance, or fear of rejection. Sometimes you have to be the one to initiate connection with old friends or to grow relationships with new ones. Please don't be discouraged if you fail to get a response or if the answer is "no"; appreciate the sweet yeses and remember: it's not the number of friends you connect with that matters. Trust the Lord to place the right people in your path, ones who crave connection just like you, and rely on Him as friend.

Even as I joke "I am wildly influential among my friends," I'm exceedingly grateful for those the Lord has given me. I count them among my greatest gifts, these women who would raise the roof for me or carry me extraordinary lengths when I cannot do it myself.

CONNECTION QUESTIONS

1. Who would you like to get to know better in your circle of acquaintances? What steps can you take to make that happen?

2. Do you believe that Jesus can fulfill your every need?

3. How can you draw closer to Jesus as friend?

CONNECTION CHALLENGE

You are more wildly influential in the lives of your community than you might think! Instead of waiting for an invitation this week, plan a Girl's Night Out. It doesn't have to be fancy or expensive, and you might receive only a few "yes" responses; but if God is putting it on your heart, why not try? Here are a few ideas to get you started:

Movie Night—Meet at a local theater or watch a movie in your home.

Make and Take—Get together with friends and create something that everyone will take home, based upon your interests.

Favorite Things party—Ask everyone to bring favorite, can't-live-without items of a certain dollar value to share. For a small crowd, each person brings enough of their item(s) to give each attendee, for bigger crowds, draw names or exchange gifts white elephant style.

PRAYER

Lord, make me vulnerable in the pursuit of friendship. Open my heart to the women right in front of me. Let me do justly, love mercy, and walk humbly with You, confident in Your love for me. Let my belief in that love give me the freedom to share it with others. Help me hold my tongue, open my ears, and put someone else's desire to be heard above my own. Help me focus on the needs of my friends and be willing to accept their help when I need it.

Golden Apples

We can't create an actual universe with our words, but we can use them to build up or destroy someone else's world.

> "Death and life are in the power of the tongue, and those who love it will eat its fruits."
>
> PROVERBS 18:21 (ESV)

ENGAGE

Ask forgiveness for a way you have hurt someone with your words. Use your words today to build up a friend who is hurting.

By Kris Camealy

It seems only fair that I tell you right up front that I haven't always wielded the power of my own tongue with care. Daily, I fight the temptation and trigger-impulse I have to speak *before* I think. This has become a particularly critical effort in our current culture of social media usage, where we carry around in our pockets the ability to share our words as soon as they pop into our heads. With a few keystrokes, we can unleash seeds of kindness that will become a harvest of hope or we can poison the hearts of those who receive our words. I'm quick to remind my children that once they say something, the words are out there. They can never be recalled or erased. This is a reality that I, too, need to be reminded of occasionally.

Shortly before my daughter turned two, I began to transform our guest room into a little girl's room for her—our third child, and our first girl. At the time, I was pregnant with my fourth child, and we knew we'd need the crib before long.

Once the walls were painted the perfect shade of "ballet slipper pink," I unrolled a set of wall stickers I'd found that depicted a sweet nature scene with a tree, some flowers, a couple of squirrels and birds. It was magnificent, colorful, and I knew my little girl would love it. I spent a good hour arranging each piece of the scene in just the right place, smoothing out the bubbles, assuring a neat presentation. When it was finished I sat back and admired the little one-dimensional menagerie pressed up there against the soft pink. It felt like the perfect finish for this playful new space. After two weeks of working late into the night, her "big girl" room was finished. I couldn't wait to show it to my daughter the next morning.

The following day, we called her to the door of her new bedroom. "Are you ready?" I asked her, brimming with anticipation. Her little blonde head nodded in agreement. I opened the door slowly, revealing her new, personalized space. Wandering in, she began chattering about the big bed, and the toys arranged neatly. She loved the ruffled curtains and the new bright yellow floral quilt.

Everywhere she turned there was something lovely to behold, something special selected specifically for her. Seeing her joy over the labors of my love brought deep joy to my heart.

Outside of our home, we don't often have the opportunity to create something of physical beauty for others. Have you ever considered that our words can be just as generous? Even with my daughter and her new room, I watched and carefully used my words to highlight and encourage the details I knew she would love. Speaking in kindness, offering encouragement, and calling out the good we see in others creates a generous space for hearts in need to find hope and joy. Of course, the opposite is also true. We can lob words like grenades, destroying the hope and happiness of others.

One day, just days into this new transition, I went in to get my daughter from her nap only to find her peeling pieces of the woodland scene off of her wall, laying them out on the carpet. Anger immediately seized my heart. "What are you doing?" I bellowed. She sat motionless at my feet, clearly stunned by my inflamed display of emotion. She had meant no harm, but only wanted to "play" with the flat characters. I took her accidental destruction personally and lashed harshly at her with my tongue.

Isn't this what happens when we speak without thinking? Our self-focus can blind us, making it nearly impossible to consider another's perspective. Without a care, we can blast our thoughts out at others, like an unwelcome gust of wind that slams doors in its wake.

OUR SELF-FOCUS CAN BLIND US, MAKING IT NEARLY IMPOSSIBLE TO CONSIDER ANOTHER'S PERSPECTIVE.

"Why would you do this?" I continued to rail. My little one dissolved into tears. I don't remember everything I said, but as my tirade about her foolishness and ingratitude spewed out, I clearly remember her shrinking before my wild eyes. Knowing myself, I'm pretty sure I gave her the long litany about how hard I had worked to make this beautiful space for her, and here she was tearing it apart piece by piece. I berated her with harsh words and an angry tone, several decibels too loud. I was incredulous, and she was crushed.

Moments later I collapsed in a shame-filled heap in the hall outside of her room. I held my face and sobbed, stunned by how heinously I had behaved. My tongue had flapped wildly in my mouth, lashing my little two-year-old with an irrational measure of harshness and hurtful words.

We don't always get a do-over with people. My daughter would go on to forgive me, and God would give me an opportunity to redeem myself in her eyes. But outside of our homes the decimation caused by ugly words doesn't always afford us the same mercy. In our communities (both online and in real life), we don't always get another chance to say the right things. Gossip about a neighbor or acquaintance can end a relationship before it even begins. Speaking out of our ignorance or judgment can build walls between us and our neighbors of other faiths and worldviews.

The book of Proverbs is full of multiple warnings about how we use our words and the power of the tongue. And for good reason. If we've ever been on the receiving end of harsh, hurtful words, we know the sting of their impact. The expression about sticks and stones being less painful than words is utterly false. While a broken bone heals, most of the time, without any residual pain, the cuts that hurtful words make in our hearts impact us long into our future. Worse, not only do we bear the pain of those words, but we often wield them against others out of our own places of woundedness. If we are not careful, the lashes of the tongue can become an unintended legacy.

That day all those years ago, in a moment of disappointment and frustration, I chose death. I tore away at the tender heart of my own child because my heart was a hotbed of unresolved anger and hurt, and I could not manage to bridle my tongue (or my emotions). God used that episode in my daughter's room to reveal a gaping hole in my own heart. Luke 6:45 reads, "His mouth speaks from the overflow of the heart." The angry words I spouted at my girl that day came from a heart that was aching and angry at things other than some silly wall stickers. I realized almost immediately after the incident that my words had damaged not only my girl's heart, but my own as well. That's what sin does—it leaves a wake of damage in its path.

The tongue is not an independent member of our body—the words that we say reveal the inner murmurings of our heart. If our hearts are hurting, and laden with anger, fear, resentment, or malice, our words will betray the secrecy of carrying these things in the hidden places. But the same is true for when our hearts are full of joy, hope, and faithfulness. *Death and life are in the power of the tongue.* We have the capacity for building or destroying, depending on the shape of our hearts. Good stewardship of our words begins in our homes amongst those we know and love, but it must also be practiced in our various communities as well. I would give anything to go back and undo the hurt and heartbreak that I caused my daughter that day.

We have the capacity for building or destroying, depending on the shape of our hearts.

Not long after this terrible moment, a friend called to catch up, and as our phone call wound to a close, she asked how she could be in prayer for me. After I'd shared with her what had happened and rattled off a handful of things weighing on my heart, she proceeded to speak the most generous, affirming words over me that I'd heard in a long while. Her words oozed grace. She reminded me about the forgiveness that comes with confession and repentance. With every breath, she built up my heart, encouraging me, inspiring me, naming my strengths, and challenging me in the hard things. Tears pooled in my eyes as I listened, hanging on to her every word. Then, as if that hadn't been enough, she proceeded to pray generously on my behalf. After we hung up the phone, I sat there at my table for a few minutes, teary, overwhelmed by the goodness that had just filled my heart. I didn't feel like I deserved those words, but she spoke life into places in my spirit that were dry and parched from struggle.

I don't know if you have had a friend or loved one bless you like this (I hope that you have), but if you haven't, imagine being wrapped in a warm blanket on a cold night. That's what it felt like sitting under the shower of those words. Her words helped me feel God's forgiveness. Our phone call was brief, but even now I can still taste the sweetness of her kindness. Mother Teresa said, "Kind words can be short and easy to speak, but their echoes are truly end-less."[19] What are the words we are speaking into our communities? What will the people we meet hear after they have met us? When I get quiet, the kind words of my friend are the words to which I want to cling. What words echo in your heart when it's quiet?

I think it's significant that the creation story begins with a fantastical demonstration of the power of words. God could have created the heavens and earth out of anything, but He chose to use His words, spoken into the void. With a word, God lit the heavens (Gen. 1:3). With a few more words, He created the horizon, water, dry land, plants, sea life, fruit, animals, days, stars—life called into existence from the throat of the Almighty. He further blessed this work by calling it all *good*. Right from the beginning, God demonstrated the positive, life-giving power of words; and then He gifted *us* with language. And this gift carries a lot of power.

We can't create an actual, physical universe with our words, but we can sure use them to build up or destroy someone else's world. Every day we encounter people in our communities who could use a few kind words. In Ephesians 5, Paul calls us imitators of God— *follow God's example*, he says. This is a tall order for those of us who struggle with taming our tongues. I fall short every single day. But still, this is to be our aim. If we say we love God, but our throat is an open grave, then we betray our witness and spread darkness—we bring death, rather than life and light. Thankfully, Scripture teaches us how to use our words. In the book of Ephesians, Paul tells us to "speak the truth in love," for this is how we grow up in Christ (Eph. 4:15). Speak truth, speak lovingly. Proverbs 16:24 (ESV) calls gracious words a "honeycomb" that bring sweetness and health to the body. Gracious words are restorative for a soul that hurts.

Every day we encounter people in our communities who could use a few kind words.

Reading these passages, I ache for the times my words have been more like vinegar than honey. Proverbs 25:11 likens rightly used words to apples of gold set in silver. What a stunning visual. I can imagine the shine of such a thing. It doesn't take much to cut someone off at the knees or close a door in their face. One ugly comment. One bit of biting sarcasm. One ill-intended joke. Criticism, thinly veiled behind a backward compliment. Our words have power—for better or worse. Words give meaning, identify, and call out. It's no wonder Scripture cautions us about how we use our words.

After I had a good hard cry on the other side of my daughter's door, I went back in and knelt down beside her. Both of our faces puffy and red from our tears, gathering her into my arms, I apologized profusely. I owned my wrongful behavior and told her how special and precious she is to me, and that I loved her desperately, but that I had done a poor job of showing her. I sought her forgiveness. She humbled me by her quick-to-forgive nature. This was *not* a shining moment of parenting. Even as I recall the memory, I still feel the sting of shame. It breaks my heart to know that my toxic words could be the very ones echoing in my daughter's heart when it's quiet.

Taming my tongue is a daily battle I have to fight. Our communities are full of hurting people who have been marginalized by thoughtless language, labels, and assumptive conversations about their identity. Wisely used words can facilitate healing and reconciliation. The gentle, kind words my friend spoke to me over the phone are an example I use to remind myself of the power of words.

Someone once said, "Words are seeds that do more than blow around. They land in our hearts and not the ground. Be careful what you plant and careful what you say. You might have to eat what you planted one day."[20] There's a reason Scripture often compares the tongue to a weapon—our words have the power to bring life or death. Whichever we choose, we will eat the fruit.

CONNECTION QUESTIONS

1. God's Word has a lot to say about taming the tongue and how we speak. What common themes about the tongue do you see in these passages like Proverbs 21:23; Psalm 141:3; and Matthew 15:11?

2. Can you recall a time when you spoke harshly to someone? What were the circumstances?

3. If taming your tongue is a struggle for you, what are some ways you can learn to slow down before speaking, to communicate your feelings in a gentle, respectful manner? Is there a friend you can ask to be an accountability partner for you as you seek to grow out of this struggle?

PRAYER

Lord God, thank You for the gift of words and the beauty of language. Help me to steward my words well, to honor You and others with my speech. Jesus, reveal to me the places where I am harboring anger or hurt or grief in my heart, so that I might speak out of the overflow of grace and kindness, the fruits of Your indwelling Holy Spirit. Teach me to tame my tongue, and use my words to build others up. In Jesus' name, amen.

CONNECTION CHALLENGE

Examine the words you have used recently. Have they been spoken in love? Consider the people you encounter every day—at the store, your work, in your home, online—how can you speak life into the hearts of the people in these communities? Who are the people around you that need to hear a good word?

Ask forgiveness for a way you have hurt someone with your words. Use your words today to build up your community, especially those who are hurting or in need of some "golden apples."

Loving Beyond the Gate

CONSIDER

Love is seeing and appreciating the reflection of God Himself in all who bear His image, no matter where they are in the world.

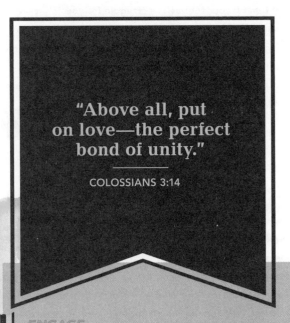

"Above all, put on love—the perfect bond of unity."

COLOSSIANS 3:14

ENGAGE

Serve in a way that has an international impact.

By Kate Motaung

I heard the familiar clinking against the metal gate at the end of our driveway. Peering through the window, I saw her standing on the sidewalk. Waiting.

She came fairly often—maybe once or twice a month. Most times, it was inconvenient. I usually had a pot of boiling water on the stove or kids in the bathtub. Sometimes I jumped up to greet her; too often, I exhaled a loud sigh. I saw her as a nuisance. An interruption.

Every time Angela showed up, there was less of her. Tattered clothes hung loose from her body like the dark circles under her eyes. Her face was as worn and tired as her baggy shirt. She smiled weakly, but her eyes were sad. Pleading. Desperate. And I saw myself reflected in Angela's eyes—pleading and desperate. Standing at the gate of the King of kings, begging for a handout.

She came asking for food, a common occurrence in our suburb just outside Cape Town, South Africa. Growing up in small-town, midwest America, I rarely even locked my front door. There was certainly no metal fence surrounding our property. But South African culture and crime rates told me I needed a gate. My own self-made culture of fear kept it closed.

Whenever Angela appeared, I asked her to wait outside the gate while I rushed back to my kitchen to see what I could spare. I packed a plastic bag full of non-perishables and fresh fruit, and prayed that God would provide spiritual food just as much as He used me to give her rice and apples.

I walked back to the end of the driveway and raised the plastic bag over the gate. Angela's hand reached up in gratitude. And I saw my own hand reaching up. Needy. Begging for grace from above. So very aware that the only reason I had anything in my cupboard to give was because God gave to me first. The only way I had any love to share was because God loved me first (1 John 4:19).

I smiled and wished Angela well, the metal gate still closed between us. A nagging question bit at my insides: Was I really

loving her? Or merely appeasing her request so I could get on with "more important" things? I was serving Angela and showing her kindness, but I felt no real connection to her. She took the bag of food and walked away, and I could pat myself on the back for doing my good deed that day.

What would have happened if I had opened the gate? What if I had humbled myself, helped her to see we were standing on the same side? Maybe then she would have seen my God, who humbled Himself, opening the gate and standing on my side of heaven.

Why didn't I invite her in? What if I had boiled the kettle and brewed some tea? Would she have seen Jesus, who invites us to come in and sit at His table? God doesn't keep the gate closed at the end of the driveway. He hears us knocking and He opens wide, that we may come in and dine with Him to our heart's desire.

Before I could love my neighbor, I had to realize how much God loves me. This whole chain reaction is set off by Love Himself—the eternal flame who ignites the burning desire to spread love like wildfire.

In the first three years of my marriage, my South African husband and I worked in full-time college student ministry in Cape Town. During that time we raised our own financial support. We were completely dependent on gifts and donations from other people. God gave us generous, faithful supporters from South Africa as well as the United States. Getting money from the US to South Africa wasn't always easy, or predictable. One particular month there was a glitch in the transfer of funds, and the money was significantly delayed. We managed to pay for rent, electricity, and gas, but ran out of money before buying groceries. The food in our fridge dwindled.

A South African couple who supported us regularly heard about our plight. The wife, Beth, called me one afternoon and announced, "I'm taking you grocery shopping. Make your list. I'll be there soon to pick you up."

An hour later, Beth and I walked side by side through the store aisles, filling our carts with milk, bread, and eggs; pasta and ground beef; chicken, rice and vegetables. As my cart overflowed, so did my heart—overcome by this tangible act of love.

Love is being willing to inconvenience yourself for the sake of another— and finding joy in it.

Love is hard work. It comes with a cost. Love is being willing to inconvenience yourself for the sake of another—and finding joy in it. Beth could have stayed home and texted the generic, "I'll pray for you," or even slipped extra money into my bank account for me to shop on my own. Instead, she loved beyond the confines of comfort. She opened the gate. She scaled the wall of inconvenience and climbed over my own fence of pride. Beth chose to inconvenience herself for the sake of connection. Rather than taking the easy path and keeping her distance, she chose to walk by my side. She paved a road that not only deepened our friendship—it led me to Jesus.

Nearly every time I slowed my car at a Cape Town intersection they were there, palms up. Beggars lingered at traffic lights, soliciting money from any who were willing to give. At first I showed compassion, rolling down my window and offering spare change from my purse. But over time my heart grew calloused from the consistent stream of need. I stopped giving. Worse, I stopped caring. Instead of smiling and handing out coins, I started to ignore the imploring faces at my window. "But, Mom!" my kids complained. "They're hungry!" Excuses flowed from my lips. "I know, but if I give them money, they probably won't use it wisely, and they'll still be here tomorrow, asking for more."

Then God reminded me of Beth's kindness in taking me shopping. He helped me realize I was failing to obey one of the two most important commands of God. When Jesus was asked, "Which is the greatest commandment?" He replied: "'Love the Lord your God with all your heart and with all your soul and with all your mind.' This is the first and greatest commandment. And the second is like it: 'Love your neighbor as yourself.' All the Law and the Prophets hang on these two commandments" (Matt. 22:36–40 NIV).

"Love your neighbor as yourself." Some might read this and ask, "Who is my neighbor?" but when I hear it, the first question that comes to mind is, "How do I love myself?" By praying for myself and hoping for the best? No. I feed myself, bathe myself, clothe myself. "Suppose a brother or a sister is without clothes and daily food," James wrote. "If one of you says to them, 'Go in peace; keep warm and well fed,' but does nothing about their physical needs, what good is it?" (James 2:15–16 NIV).

Convicted, I changed my ways at the traffic lights. Rather than fixing my gaze on the red light, I smiled, cracked open my window, and greeted the beggars. I apologized for not having anything to give, but said I hoped to see them again. I started buying an extra loaf of bread at the store to give away as I drove home. Sometimes I kept a bag of apples in the car to place in the open hands that reached for my window as I waited for a green light.

Most of all, I made an effort to smile and look them in the eye. I asked their names, showed them they were noticed. That they mattered. Because love doesn't always look like giving money or food. Sometimes it looks like making eye contact, because Love is the God who sees. Sometimes it looks like listening intently to the story of someone's heart—because Love is the God who hears. Sometimes love looks like calling a person by name—because God not only sees and hears, He calls you and me by name. Love is seeing and appreciating the reflection of God Himself in all who bear His image.

We might not have material goods to give away, but may we never be accused of being stingy with love.

After moving back to suburban America, I no longer met beggars at traffic lights. I didn't have people knocking on my gate asking for food. In fact, I lived in a neighborhood where most people kept to themselves. I had to intentionally seek out ways to connect with others. Maybe you don't have people knocking on your door. But every time you pour lemonade into plastic cups for the neighbor kids playing in your backyard, you serve Jesus. Every time you wipe sticky fingers and tables, you serve Jesus. Whatever you do for the least of these, you do for the King of kings (Matt. 25:34–40).

Maybe for you, love looks like:

- Visiting the widowed lady next door. I wonder what would happen if you offered to read to her for an hour a week, or asked her to read to your kids.
- Inviting the military wife from your church over to cook supper together—perhaps even a cooking marathon where you prepare several freezer meals all at once.
- Asking an international student to come for lunch after the Sunday morning service, or to your daughter's soccer game on Saturday.

- Inviting a small group of college ladies over for dinner.
- Looking for ways to encourage a coworker who has been acting different or unusually difficult to be around.

SOMETIMES THE SMALLEST GESTURES, WHEN DONE OUT OF LOVE, SPEAK THE LOUDEST.

It doesn't have to be complex—sometimes the smallest gestures, when done out of love, speak the loudest.

My interactions with Angela in South Africa led me to ask the questions, "What other gates have I built for myself? The wall of pride? Of independence? Of inconvenience? What keeps me from loving the way God commands? How can I reach beyond those fences, past those walls?"

How can we love beyond the gate? How can we love beyond the gates of racial differences, of country borders, of economic brackets?

No matter where in the world we live, loving beyond the gate means building genuine, meaningful relationships. The kind that reach deeper than surface level. Why? Because relationship-building is road-building. When we cultivate relationships, we lay down bricks of trust, and those bricks pave the way for Jesus. They cement His truth and smooth the path for others to follow, to tread the narrow way, to step into His kingdom.

We crave connection because we're made in the image of God. The Father, Son, and Holy Spirit have perfect fellowship with each other. They're *one*. That was Jesus' prayer for us, too—that we may "become perfectly one" (John 17:23 ESV). Why? So the world may know that the Father sent Jesus, and that God loves the world even as He loves His own Son. So really, it's all about love—God's immeasurable love for us, and our overflowing gratitude to Him.

But love is risky business. It's far easier to fix our gaze straight ahead, to ignore those standing in the gravel on the shoulder of the road. It's easy to build fences and locked gates around our hearts.

Because to connect is to be vulnerable—and I'm not sure I'm ready to go there. So instead, I keep the gate of my heart closed and lift my offerings over the fence. That way I'm not exposed. I won't get hurt.

But that's not how God works. He's in the business of opening gates, tearing down barriers, breaking down walls. He even sent His only Son to finish the work, "for he himself is our peace, who has made the two groups one and has destroyed the barrier, the dividing wall of hostility" (Eph. 2:14 NIV). God didn't withhold His love from us for the sake of protecting His own heart. He "did not spare his own Son, but gave him up for us all" (Rom. 8:32 NIV).

In Colossians 3:12 (NIV), the apostle Paul tells us who we are in Christ. If you love Jesus, you are one of "God's chosen people, holy and dearly loved." Did you catch that? In Christ, you are *chosen. Holy. Dearly loved.*

> *God is in the business of opening gates, tearing down barriers, and breaking down walls.*

And as God's chosen, holy, dearly loved people, we have a special wardrobe. Paul tells us to "clothe yourselves with compassion, kindness, humility, gentleness and patience. Bear with each other and forgive one another if any of you has a grievance against someone. Forgive as the Lord forgave you. And over all these virtues put on love, which binds them all together in perfect unity" (Col. 3:12–14 NIV).

I don't often think about putting on love—but this world is a cold place. Just as I wouldn't dream of stepping outside in January without my jacket, neither should I dream of getting out of bed without putting on love, each and every day. It may require significant effort, but Lord, may we never grow weary of putting on love—even and especially when people knock on my gate at the most inconvenient times.

When I think back to my encounters with Angela in South Africa, I wonder: Did she see me wearing love, or irritation? Whether at the end of our driveways or in the grocery store, we have a choice: to clothe ourselves with the love of Christ, or to stay hidden behind the walls we've built. Though it requires significant effort, may we never grow weary of putting on love.

CONNECTION QUESTIONS

1. What walls have you built for yourself? How do they keep you from loving well?

2. How is God prompting you to love beyond the gate?

3. What is one practical step you can take to remind yourself to "put on love" every morning?

CONNECTION CHALLENGE

We can reach out to people and organizations doing fabulous, world-changing work. I had a needy, hungry mama knocking on my gate; many organizations do, too. And they're dedicating their lives to putting on love—because God loved them first.

Serve in a way that has an international impact. Some suggestions: volunteer with refugees; host an international student; go on a short-term missions trip; send care packages to a missionary family; or buy merchandise from Fair Trade companies.

A Recipe for Community

Just as each ingredient in a recipe is necessary, every member in Christ's body has a special function.

> "Now as we have many parts in one body, and all the parts do not have the same function, in the same way we who are many are one body in Christ and individually members of one another."
>
> ROMANS 12:4–5

ENGAGE

Spend time with your pastor or small group leader and ask questions to learn their story—discover how, even in our differences, we are all still very much the same.

I tie an apron around my waist and pick up a spatula. The front of my classroom looks more like a cooking show than an English class. Ingredients, like flour and sugar and cream of tartar, are spread across the table. I've set out measuring spoons, rolling pins, and mixing bowls too.

Even though I arranged the desks differently today, I notice the same cluster of girls clumped together. Some things in seventh grade never change.

But the strange set-up captures everyone's attention.

"Who loves chocolate chip cookies?"

Hands go up.

"How about sugar cookies?"

More hands.

"My favorite cookies are snickerdoodles," I say, "and I thought it might be fun to talk about cookies today instead of grammar."

The cheers can be heard down the hall.

With a measuring cup I scoop the flour and sift it into a large glass bowl.

"Has anyone ever tasted flour? By itself?"

I take a spoonful of flour, as if to inspect it closely, then I swallow it whole and nearly choke on the dryness of it. My students giggle while poofs of white puffy clouds float from the corners of my mouth. I need to guzzle almost an entire water bottle to wash down the flour.

"Bleh. It's awful by itself. Well, what about vanilla extract? It smells so good. Anybody ever try it?"

I hold the small brown bottle for my students in the front row to catch a sweet whiff. Yum. But as soon as I drink a teaspoon of vanilla extract, a sour expression distorts my face and my whole body quivers in reaction.

"Okay. Don't try that at home. It's pretty nasty."

I continue to taste each ingredient—admittedly, with theatrical flair—then pour each one into the bowl while my students have a good laugh. There's something amusing about watching your English teacher torture herself. I even gulp a raw egg.

The kids nearly explode, "Ewww!"

But we eventually get to the good stuff. Sugar and butter. And the best part? Chocolate chips. I pass around an extra bag so everyone can enjoy a few dark morsels of goodness.

"What would happen if we left out all the yucky parts? You know, the cream of tartar and the vanilla extract? What if we only made cookies with sugar and chocolate chips?"

I write *rhetorical question* on the board because we already know the answer: The recipe won't work without all the ingredients.

I gesture toward the table, "How are all these ingredients a little bit like grammar?"

Silence settles. So I eat a few more chocolate chips. Waiting. Munching. Smiling.

A lone hand goes up, and a quiet girl from the back row says, "Are the ingredients like the parts of speech?"

I nod. "How many of you just love studying grammar?" Groans fill the room. "Yeah, I know. It's another rhetorical question. Learning about nouns and verbs and conjunctions might not be the most exciting part of English class, but we know what happens when we put them all together. We get to read stories of adventure and plot twists full of mystery."

Eventually, the bell rings and my students file out the door, so I gather my things while thinking about the gross stuff I swallowed, seriously regretting the raw egg. My students enjoyed the theatrics, but I pray God will plant other seeds in their hearts as well. Because the same analogy is true in a lot of ways.

The girls who always sit together don't realize there are other girls in the class who would like to join them. I see it on their faces. Deep down hoping. Perhaps for an invitation. To sit together. To talk together. To be together.

I remember feeling the same way at their age. On Friday nights my whole town would show up for the high school football game. I would go too, but I preferred to watch the cheerleaders. They looked like septuplets. Everything they wore matched perfectly, right down to their purple and gold shoelaces. I especially liked the dance routines they performed at halftime. Something inside me longed to be one of them. And I convinced myself that if I could join their squad, if I could wear the same pleated skirt and the same V-neck vest, I would finally feel like I belonged.

So when tryouts were announced at the end of the school year, I tried out for the squad, and I made it. My background in dance paid off. I was in!

I imagined the group of seven happily becoming a group of eight. Me, the newest member of the cheer team. Every day for two hours after school, I practiced with the squad and memorized all the routines. But the cheerleaders all talked to each other, and they wouldn't talk to me. I felt invisible in their midst. At every football game I stood among them—wearing an identical uniform, cheering for the same team, looking so similar, yet knowing I wasn't really one of them.

The pain of their rejection etched deep. My first year of cheerleading became my last. Everything inside me wanted to go back to being the girl who hid in the crowd, pretending it didn't matter.

But it did.

Decades later I realize the desire to belong never really goes away. We crave connection like we crave chocolate. I think a seventh grade girl still lingers somewhere inside all of us, longing for purple and gold shoelaces.

Maybe for you it was never a cheerleading squad. Maybe it was something else. The groups may change, but the pain doesn't. Today it might be a group of women at work who go out to lunch together. Or the moms of littles who plan a play-date together. Or the women at Bible study who like to sit together.

Maybe for you it's the Welcome Card at church that asks you to check a box saying you're "single" or "divorced" or "widowed." The small box forces you into an even smaller category, when all you want is a place to belong. As is. For who you really are.

We know we were made for community, but fitting in doesn't always come easy.

Our situations may be different, but our hearts experience rejection the same. We know we were made for community, but fitting in doesn't always come easy. For a long time I couldn't figure out why the other cheerleaders didn't accept me. I wore the same things. I made the same moves. I did everything I could to be just like them. But I learned the hard way that true community doesn't come from looking the same and acting the same. I'm different. And so are you. We're supposed to be.

True community is fostered in an environment where everyone is encouraged to be whom God made them to be—when the God-given differences that make each person unique are celebrated and welcomed. Because every person has something special to offer. God placed inside every human soul a purpose that no one else can fulfill. And He gave every person the gifts needed to accomplish that purpose.

IT'S ONLY WHEN WE FULFILL OUR PURPOSE IN CHRIST THAT WE FIND TRUE CONTENTMENT.

It's only when we fulfill our purpose in Christ that we find true contentment.

All of creation reveals God's heart for variety. Every bird that sings. Every fish that swims. Every insect that crawls. Each one is unique in size, shape, and color. God obviously wants it that way. He enjoys diversity. So should we.

This is why I've loved participating in choir at church. In choir, we come together from many different backgrounds. The youngest is fifteen, the oldest is in her nineties. We are young. We are old. We are single. We are married. We are rich. We are poor. We are broken. We are whole. Yet we sing and worship together. All ages. All backgrounds.

The beauty of God-designed diversity is most evident in heart-devoted unity.

The beauty of God-designed diversity is most evident in heart-devoted unity.

I think of my students. Each one is gifted in an exceptional way. Brandon likes to sit by the window. He doodles on his notepad, but his doodles always turn into something amazing. He's an artist through and through. Jadyn likes to make others feel welcome. She has a way of noticing the quieter ones in the room. And Eric likes to read Shakespeare out loud with a silly accent. He makes everyone laugh and lightens the room with a little fun.

Just as each ingredient in a recipe is necessary, every member in Christ's body has a special function.

A cookie has many ingredients, but together they form a savory dessert.

A book has many elements, but together they make a wonderful story.

A choir has many voices, but together they create a beautiful harmony.

We're different from each other for a reason. God wants us to serve in different ways, so He gives each person a unique purpose; and together, we can serve the way God intended. Because every member in Christ's body is essential. No one person is more important than another. Every person, and every function, is necessary. Some of us may serve in visible ways, while others of us may serve in hidden ways, but all of us are needed. In this way, we belong to each other. Because we need each other.

We are many parts, but one body in Christ. This has been God's intention all along. He called us into His family and created the church—a place where everyone has a part to sing, or a part to play. A place where the focus is purely on magnifying Him.

With each new day I want to embrace the vast array of experiences that come my way—both good and bad, sweet and sour. Because it all comes together to form something so much better than I could ever imagine on my own. I want to create an atmosphere in my classroom where my students know they belong, just as they are. And I want my daily life to look a little more like my choir, with variety and color.

The Master Chef has had this recipe for community in mind since before the beginning of time. A recipe to bring His people together, from California to Connecticut to Calcutta.

God's plan is to rescue and redeem us. To give us hope and a future. And He gave us the greatest Recipe Book ever, full of His instructions, to guide us every step of the way.

We can begin today.

What if we prayed for someone we think we couldn't possibly have much in common with?

What if we struck up a conversation with someone in line behind us at a local coffee shop?

What if we intentionally sought out someone in our church who seems very different from us?

It might sound crazy. A little different for sure. Sort of like an English teacher talking about cookies and ingredients. But something inside me warms at the idea. And I'm pretty sure the thought of it makes His heart glad too.

CONNECTION QUESTIONS

1. Can you recall a time when you wanted to fit in, but for whatever reason, it just didn't work out? What did you learn from that experience?

2. Is there someone you come in contact with on a casual basis whom you could befriend in a deeper way?

3. What is the special ingredient that you bring to the recipe for community?

CONNECTION CHALLENGE

Who in your life could benefit from the gift of an invitation? There are people all around us who do not understand the value they bring as unique individuals. Ask the Lord to open your eyes to your immediate surrounding; the place where you begin and end most days; the street you drive on a regular basis, waving to the same people as you drive.

Or spend time with your pastor or small group leader and ask questions to learn their story—your encouragement could be just the thing they need. Discover how, even in our differences, we're all still very much the same.

PRAYER

Lord, You created us to connect, to be in relationship, with You and with others. Forgive us when we're tempted to stay in our comfortable, familiar circles. Help us to step out in courage to connect with someone we don't know, especially someone we wouldn't typically know. Open our eyes to see others the way You see us all. May we embrace the unique purpose You've given each of us and celebrate our differences as well as our likenesses. For we're all made in Your wondrous and glorious image. And You are good and holy and true. Amen.

Mighty Acts

Sharing how God comes through daily and in the big-need moments encourages others when they want to give up.

"One generation will declare Your works to the next and will proclaim Your mighty acts."

PSALM 145:4

ENGAGE

Set up a schedule to remember to pray for your family and community by setting your phone alarm throughout the day.

By Stephanie Bryant

Y ou might call it Girls' Night Out. My husband calls them Hen Parties. Whatever the name, it's been far too long since I've had one, and I miss spending time with my friends. I'm in the throes of parenting a toddler while my husband travels extensively for work. We also have a small, ten-acre farm with chickens and a lot of dreams to plant.

I thoroughly enjoy my life, but I haven't done a very adequate job of hosting friends or keeping in touch or drawing near to other women, whether in the same season as me or not.

Connecting with friends on a "God level" may not look as big as you imagine. It may not be a women's ministry or a big party in your backyard or a conference. It may look like texting friends to check on life, praying for situations without being asked, persistently asking friends for coffee even when both your schedules are mayhem.

Sometimes drawing near to each other may start in your own family—your mom, your daughter, an aunt or grandmother. We often forget to minister to and love those God has placed in our family. Those relationships can be the hardest for some, and maybe an afterthought, thinking there are so many in need in our neighborhood or world.

I've learned the most from women that did the day-to-day with their family beautifully, humbly, and lovingly. I've been blessed to come from a line of Jesus-believing women, which I know in itself is a mighty act of God.

These women were patient and prayerful, and welcomed others to join in what God was doing in their lives. I want to be in community with women who will challenge me to love sacrificially, even when I don't feel like it.

I've been blessed to come from a long line of women who love God and have given their lives to Jesus. They serve their families without complaining and love others well. It wasn't until recently that I asked questions about what their faith lives were like growing up.

Raising my own miracle daughter, whom we prayed to conceive for seven years, has me thinking more about the faith legacy I'm leaving and how to weave His glory into the fiber of her being. I want Gabrielle to praise His name without thinking. I want her first instinct, when in a tight spot, to be prayer to the One with all the wisdom. I want her to be open handed with her "things"—money, possessions, and time. I want her to not be fearful but to listen for God's small voice leading her into His big adventure. I want Gabrielle to live in the fruit of the prayers I've prayed for her, her life a pure reflection of God's grace.

"When were you saved?" "What church did you grow up going to?" "Did your dad talk about his faith with you?" "Did you grow up reading your Bible?" "How was the subject of faith approached in your family, or did you all talk about it at all?" "How did your mom teach you about God?" These were a few of the questions I asked some of the women in my family.

Some of the conversations surprised and fascinated me. I was shocked to find most of their families didn't talk about their faith at the dinner table or when they were going to bed or on a car trip or walking to school. It was "private."

I thought to myself, "What a loss!" All of the missed opportunities to praise God for His mighty acts and awesome power with their children. The moments to invite others into a beautiful expression of love for their Savior that passed them by on a daily basis.

Honestly, I know that isn't uncommon. We go through the motions of life with family and friends, not talking about the important things, maybe not stopping to ask the hard questions. Being concerned there might be an eye roll or a cold shoulder when we do have a God conversation. Or maybe we're just embarrassed about how we haven't grown lately ourselves, so why would our children listen to us? Or we weren't raised by parents that shared about their faith or wove God into daily activities, so how would we even begin? It might feel awkward, but there is always hope.

Legacy is powerful. I had the privilege of knowing my great-grandmother Meme. She was a loving, tender, woman of God. I've never heard anyone talk about Jesus like she did. Meme knew Him like a best friend. Any time I would go over to her apartment, she was on the couch reading her Bible. Every time.

Meme talked to Jesus constantly and loved Him sweetly. Everyone knew it. And we all knew we were being prayed for.

The last ten years of her life, she was bedridden. Her mind was sharp, remembering dates and stories none of us could keep track of. But her body broke down too early. I remember visiting her and realizing she had chosen to have no TV in her room. What did she do all day?

She only had a digital clock to show her what time it was and photos of those she loved, with a large image of Jesus on the wall. She whispered to me a time—11:11. She said that was my time. Meme explained she prayed for each member of our family and friends twice a day, every time our number came up.

She's passed on to have face-to-face conversations with our Savior, but to this day I still look at the clock a couple times a week and see 11:11. I think of her, thanking God for her love of Jesus, the example she set, and the legacy of prayer I am living today.

Meme never got to meet my daughter, Gabrielle. But she prayed for her. My husband and I had been married for a few years and were already trying to have a baby when Meme passed on. I learned how to pray and listen to my Savior through those seven years of waiting for our miracle. Meme showed me how to wait on my miracle.

I remember the day God made me a mother. I was in my home office, frustrated by another well-intentioned person suggesting, "It's all in God's timing." I told God I was going to punch the next person who said those words to me. I was fed up. And frustrated with God.

I told Him so. I ugly-cried as I poured out my heart to Him and asked Him all the questions waiting women do—"Why has it not happened yet? What have I done wrong? Heal me! Help me! Why is this taking so long?!"

I got it all out. And then His small voice became louder and got in my face.

God asked me, "Do you want me to answer your prayers?"

What kind of silly question was that? Didn't I just say that? Of course I did.

God asked the same question another way, "Do you want me to answer your prayers for your child? Are you willing to wait on my perfect timing for her?"

In asking me to wait longer, to trust Him, I surrendered control of my heart toward my child and how I viewed mothering, and trusted Him for what was best. He took the pressure off of me, gave me a beautiful story of hope, and answered my prayer. I had confirmation I would become a mother—someday. His day.

WAITING CAN TURN INTO EXCITED ANTICIPATION, WHICH MAKES THE GIFT SO MUCH SWEETER AND PRECIOUS.

Waiting can turn into excited anticipation, which makes the gift so much sweeter and precious. My daughter is God's gift to me. I know all children are a gift from the Lord, He tells us as much, but Gabrielle Elise is a jewel in His crown.

Once I was pregnant, glowing in the miracle God had finally made real on earth as it was in heaven, I was getting bigger and delivery realities were setting in. I read my Bible studies out loud as I did them, talked to Gabrielle like I would a friend, and prayed the Word over her every day—still in my belly. I wanted her to love God's Word, come to know the Lord at an early age, and serve Him all the days of her life.

But I was getting a little nervous to take on the responsibility of motherhood and helping make those prayers come to fruition. God seemed to peel back the ceiling and showed me a glimpse of the eternal. I could imagine Jesus laughing, jumping over and kicking every color of balloon into the air. Confetti filled the sky with sunshine glory. It was as if His spirit was telling mine, "You think you've waited a long time for Gabrielle to come? I've been waiting even longer. This is what heaven will look like the day your daughter is born—her heavenly birthday party." I focused on this awesome moment a few months later as my doctor was doing an emergency C-section and had to save Gabrielle in sixty seconds. She came out screaming and full of life.

I share this story with Gabrielle, too. About what a miracle she is and how excited Jesus is that she was born. She reminded me the other day, "I'm a miracle, Mom." And then she told others at the store.

Gabrielle is now a toddler. She would rather read one of her Bibles and talk about Jesus or one of His miracles than play dolls or kitchen or be outside. She's a living reflection of the answers to my prayers. God reminds me often of the miracles He continues to do and how prayer can move His mighty acts.

I don't save "God stories" for when I'm trying to make a point or just in times of trouble with my daughter. I don't just pray with her at meal time. I slow down and look her in the eye and tell her about the bigger, beautiful story she's a part of, every day. We pray throughout the day as our senses prompt us—a wreck we drive by, someone at the store with a boo-boo, praising God for good news from a friend.

Now Gabrielle will lift her hands and shout "Praise God!" when the DVD player works for her favorite Bible video after stalling out. She thanks God for her puppy, Hank, and her chickens with their eggs. She asks God to help others or thanks Him for her friends.

As women, we naturally talk about someone we love. Psalm 145:4 isn't about duty or a checklist. It's not even parenting or mentoring advice. It's love advice.

When we are enamored and overwhelmed by all the beauty someone has brought into our lives, how we are made new and look at things with fresh lightness, it's second nature to tell the story of how we met, the sweet things He's done for us, or the hurdles we've overcome together.

It's really about living out these verses from Deuteronomy 6:5–9, with the help and power of the Holy Spirit.

*"Love the L*ORD *your God with all your heart and with all your soul and with all your strength. These commandments that I give you today are to be on your hearts. Impress them on your children. Talk about them when you sit at home and when you walk along the road, when you lie down and when you get up. Tie them as symbols on your hands and bind them on your foreheads. Write them on the doorframes of your houses and on your gates"* (*Deut. 6:5–9* NIV).

We did that very thing as a family of three recently. We wrote verses on the doorframes and walls of our new farmhouse as it was being framed this past summer. Some were scribbles of a two-year-old, but I walked the rooms and prayed as I wrote specific Scriptures in each room.

We are in the middle of a Jesus-led adventure on the Bryant Family Farm, seeing answers to big prayers and living in a promised land only God could orchestrate. We don't have many details of what His plan is for us on these ten acres, but we are praying for His miracles to continue in our lives.

Listening is crucial to have awe of the One we love. To pray according to God's will and see the fruit of His miracles, we must listen. We must not only share our stories of how God has come through in our daily lives and the big-need moments, but we also must hear others' stories too, of God's work to magnify His name in praise. And to encourage others when they want to give up right before the miracle arrives.

Praise God in the small and the big.

How do you cultivate meaningful community that declares God's mighty acts to the next generation? You love Jesus well and don't take your eyes off Him. Carve out time for Bible study, praying you and future generations will desire His Word. You live in the legacy created by the believer before you, or you begin the legacy for future generations of your family. You praise God in the small and the big. You say the praise out loud in all situations.

CONNECTION QUESTIONS

1. How has God protected and guided you to be the woman you are today?

2. What is a mighty act you've seen God do in your life this year?

3. What do you want your legacy to be?

CONNECTION CHALLENGE

Investing in our community doesn't need to take a lot of time, just a little planning. If you have a few minutes in your day you have time to begin to leave a lasting legacy for the community God has gifted you.

Today, try Meme's prayer times: set up a schedule for remembering to pray for particular members of your family and community by setting your phone alarm throughout the day.

PRAYER

Lord, You are welcome here, in this space. I pray that we would be overcome by Your presence in such a way that we can't help but share Your mighty acts with our friends and family. May the freedom we experience through You and in You be so overwhelmingly wonderful that we pour that legacy out onto the generations after us out of the overflow of our hearts. As we become so aware of Your presence in all of the beautiful, ordinary moments of our day, may we experience Your goodness and glory and declare without hesitation Your mighty name, Your mighty acts, and Your miraculous grace.

No Mistake

God calls us to honor one another.

"Love one another with brotherly affection. Outdo one another in showing honor."

ROMANS 12:10 (ESV)

ENGAGE

Commit to praying for your community or a specific person for seven days.

By Christine Wright

Headed west on I-10, it never failed. The storm clouds would appear about the place the land changed from level terrain to rolling hills. About an hour outside of the city I missed so much. I began to refer to that part of the state as Rainy Valley.

The original plan was to move for only a few years—then we would head back to the city. The city near my aging parents. The one where my best friend lived. The one with the beach and a real downtown and more stores than I had time to explore.

Having never made a move as an adult, except for college, it originally seemed like a compelling adventure. One we couldn't turn down. At the time, I had no way of knowing what all the "yes" and "no" answers would mean for us. We would find out the hard way as year bled into year and it became obvious we wouldn't be moving back home. Every door seemed to close on that dream. Even a few we tried to pry open. Not one would budge.

I stewed in what felt like a permanent state of "I can't stand this place!" No matter the good that was going on around me, home was never far from my thoughts. My favorite small talk question became, "So, how do you like it here?" I'd unload every negative thought I had about the city, the stores (*what stores?*), the football team (*not a fan*), the location (*no beach*), and the people who liked the city (*just why did they like living here so much?*).

It probably comes as no surprise that during these years I only called on Jesus in extreme emergencies—never outside of that. I simply didn't have a day-to-day relationship with Him. Visiting a different church here and there meant my family wasn't hearing the Word and had no one to hold us accountable. Sadly, my Bible had become buried at the bottom of a pile on my nightstand.

For the first time in my life, I had no nearby, close friends I could call on in an emergency. I had never had trouble making friends before, so that too was lumped into the pile labeled "all because of this move!" and became another reason I couldn't wait to head home.

The struggles came, one on top of another for my family. Loved ones' battles with addiction, my own tangle with encephalitis, and finally my divorce. Looking back now, I can see that through each one of those storms God was calling me home to Him, regardless of my physical location. Each time I'd start to make the turn toward Him, but it wouldn't take long and I'd be off course again, convinced my way was better. I was being led by fear and mistakenly believing it was safer to do what I had always done. It would take over a decade, and trying over and over my own way, before realizing I couldn't go it alone.

Remarried and desperate to see a lasting change in my family, I wasn't sure what to do, so I started to pray. Soon after I started praying, I found a church home. Jesus was calling me, and this time I said yes. It was in church that I came home to Him, but I came hauling my wounds and fears along with me. Baggage I was too scared to put down for good.

While still dragging those heavy bags, I met a sweet woman at our church who challenged me. I didn't know her much beyond a polite hello, but it seemed she had it together. Too together for us to ever be friends! A stellar mom, a kind wife—a Jesus girl who didn't seem so weighed down by baggage. I was fresh from a year-long battle that could best be described as a dark night of the soul. I put on a good show but felt far from stellar or kind. It was as if she was everything I wasn't, along with everything I wasn't ever going to be, so it was just easier to avoid her.

One fall day, as the Bible study we were both attending was preparing to meet again after summer break, God laid something on my heart I didn't see coming. *Pray for her.* Okay, I could do that. But the next thing He asked? *Write a card and tell her you have committed to pray for her throughout the study.* Are You kidding me, Lord? I didn't think I could do it. It may not seem like a big deal to most people, but my pride made it feel like a mountain much higher than I could ever climb. Writing that note felt like I was dying to self.

Romans 12:10 (NIV) says, "Love one another with brotherly affection. Outdo one another in showing honor." *Outdo*, according to the *Merriam-Webster Dictionary*, is defined "to go beyond in action or performance." When we "go beyond" in showing honor, we come together as the body of Christ. Sharing the good and the bad, and lifting the other one up. For me, at that time, trusting Jesus and writing that note felt too far beyond. Never mind the idea of having to explain I was praying for someone I barely knew and then hand it to her! I longed to honor God and do what He called me to do, but the wounds in my past made it nearly impossible to honor the person God called me to honor.

Then it sank in. The only way out was to go through the hard thing I didn't think was possible. God gave me the strength and the words to write, as well as the courage to follow through.

I prayed throughout the entire Bible study, and something curious happened. My heart was changed, and I saw this woman through new eyes. Rather than someone to avoid, or as a competitor, *she became a friend*. Only God! To this day she is one of my dearest friends, with whom I can pray, cry, and laugh (usually in the same conversation). Matthew Henry says it well in his commentary on Romans 12: "True Christian love will make us take part in the sorrows and joys of each other."[21] We have supported each other in prayer through the years following, through all kinds of situations God knew would be coming for both of us. He knew one day we would be standing in the gap in prayer for each other. Without the hard, holy work of laying down pride, and ultimately honoring God, I'm not sure this friendship would have happened.

Often God calls us into scary, unknown places, to the "hard holy," in order to prepare us for what's to come.

Often God calls us into scary, unknown places, to the "hard holy," in order to prepare us for what's to come. Not long after all of this happened, I felt led to start praying for the church I attended. I didn't understand it, but the Lord led me in how to pray, so I did.

Fast-forward three years to the fall of 2014. Still praying for my church, by then I was also leading a website with a group of close friends. It had begun to feel like it was time for someone else to lead the site, but the truth was too hard to face, so I did my best to ignore it. Finally, it became too strong to ignore. Heartbroken to have to lay it down, I had a distinct leading that I was being called to something local instead. That stirring to lay it down came in September of 2014.

In October, I began to make preparations for someone else to lead the site. I did what I felt God was calling me to do, but truly none of it made sense. One month later, in November, my city was hit with two tragic shootings within days of each other, one involving our local university. I felt a burden now to pray not just for my own church, but also to pray for revival for my city like never before. I was so desperate, I even began to ask people if any multi-denominational groups existed in our town that prayed together.

My heart was just broken for the city. I felt a tug to repent for all the years I had said less than honoring things, so I did. Even for the old nickname I'd given it. I repented as well for the envy I'd felt over other people's placement here and the lies I'd believed about my own.

A few weeks after the shootings, I met with two like-minded friends for coffee. In the space of an hour and a half, a plan was birthed. A way for the area churches to come together. To pray for revival in our city, state, nation, and world. Strangely simple, it was a plan only God could have come up with.

Just like that, we began to meet monthly for non-denominational revival prayer meetings. People from many different churches, gathering together for a time of worship and prayer. We have continued ever since.

My favorite part of those meetings comes at the end. After having sung, prayed, laughed, and cried, the transformation is evident. Standing in the same place where strangers stood less than an hour before, now stand friends. They stand together as the body of Christ. Not promoting or competing. Not tearing down or destroying, rather having joined their voices in prayer for the city where the Lord has placed them.

God calls us to honor one another in our local church, as well as beyond. Mark 3:25 tells us, "If a house is divided against itself, that house cannot stand." For so long, we haven't honored one another nor come together in unity. We have competed with each other, with various programs and for numbers. We have believed the lies of the enemy. For me, those lies were the years I spent convinced I was in this city by mistake. Those lies also roared each time I compared myself to someone I met. When I convinced myself we were more different than we were alike.

Even in the revival prayer meetings, we have been guilty of falling for the lies. We've looked around and caught ourselves in the numbers game. Thinking there weren't enough people in attendance at a meeting. We have had to remind each other it's not about the numbers. It's about the body of Christ coming together, regardless of what that looks like, or what the numbers may communicate from a worldly perspective.

When we are driven by the noise of the world saying we must keep up and keep going, everything becomes a competition. It's the hard driving voice saying it's up to us to make our own way. That there's not enough in the world, and we need to compete for the little that's available. As we read God's Word and pray, He will sort the truth from the lies. His voice is the gentle reminder that ultimately we are not alone.

More important than a physical location, it is when we finally return home to Jesus that He enables us to do the hard work He calls us to. To drop the baggage we've been dragging and pray the prayers He writes on our hearts. Ones that stretch us beyond our comfort zones, calling us to lift others up, both inside and outside of our churches. Rather than feel the pressure of an envy-driven competition, we begin to truly have a heart for where God has planted us. We notice our unique place on the wall and begin to do the work necessary to see real change come in our lives and in the lives of those around us. Instead of constantly comparing our story with others and wishing and praying our lives were different, we realize we are not here by mistake but have been strategically planted. We are able to bless others, share in their sorrows, and even pray for those who have hurt us.

Jesus has a plan for us, wherever we are. Let us return home to Him and honor each other.

CONNECTION QUESTIONS

1. Who can you think of that needs Romans 12:10 prayed for them? Your family? Your church? The schools in your city?

2. When was a time you felt God calling you to do something challenging? What was the result?

3. What is one thing that makes it especially difficult to "count others more significant" than ourselves?

CONNECTION CHALLENGE

Is there a group in your community, or a specific person, you have not always treated with honor in the past? Has God brought them to mind as you read today? Pray and confess your thoughts or actions to God today and be open to any action God asks you to take.

Commit to praying for that part of your community or your specific person for at least seven days, asking God to bless them and to guide you as you pray for them.

PRAYER

Dear Lord, we confess the times that we have slipped into envy-driven competition. Show us the lies we have believed and flood our hearts with Your truth. Help us to outdo one another in showing honor (Rom. 12:10). We lift up our families, friends, and communities to You as well and pray that You would bless them abundantly. Show us how best to honor them. Thank You for the city you have planted each one of us in. We trust we are not here by accident and pray that You would show us our unique giftings and put us to work however You see fit. Lord, we pray for revival in our churches and cities and that it would start with each of us. It is in Your name, Jesus, we pray, amen.

A Grand Blueprint for Hospitality

There is no grand blueprint for biblical hospitality apart from simply loving others.

"Be hospitable to one another without complaining. Based on the gift each one has received, use it to serve others, as good managers of the varied grace of God."

1 PETER 4:9–10

ENGAGE

Gather your family or friends together and make room at the table for some new friends God is bringing into your lives.

By Jen Schmidt

As I ran to stop the closing metal door, I struggled to maneuver our double stroller through the opening. Bumping on one side, then the other, it finally came to its resting point amid the packed elevator. Apologizing to the others, my eyes glanced down at our elder son, giggling from his mini bumper car ride.

A Saturday night out on the town, even to window shop at the local mall, was worth every chaotic adventure that came with two boys under two—and I craved a night out. Three weeks earlier we had said good-bye to family, jobs, our church home, and a lifetime of shared memories as we completed a life-changing move from Wisconsin to North Carolina.

So many emotions ran rampant during this transitional time; exhausted, homesick, and isolated, I knew we had been called to North Carolina, but I still struggled with starting all over. My husband greeted the young family standing next to us and noted the dad's Steelers shirt. Yes, there's something about men and their hometown football allegiances because by the time the elevator doors opened three floors later, our guys had bonded over exchanged Packers and Steelers stories.

We waved good-bye and went our separate ways, until the next morning.

As we picked up our toddler from his new Sunday school classroom, we saw our elevator acquaintances across the hall. I could not believe it. What were the chances?

In those next moments, their actions marked the way I'd define and live out hospitality for years to come. Without any preplanning or overthinking, without taking time to worry if their home was clean or if they had a meal ready to go, they extended an invitation to relative strangers.

I'll never forget when they crossed the hall and asked, "I know it's last minute and we just met, but would your family like to come over for lunch today?"

Today? Right now? I was stunned; stunned, grateful, and overwhelmed by this simple act of kindness, a symbolic lifeline extended when I most needed it. Our new friends' home was humble. They lived off a sole public school teacher's salary, so there were no extras, yet we gathered lunch meat for sandwiches and made boxed pasta to stretch the meal. That afternoon, their hearts rolled out the red carpet, and their giving hospitality welcomed us into community.

Two decades have passed since that meal, and that simple exchange became a remembrance marker of sorts, a tangible demonstration of God's love to me. In a time when I felt so alone, He knew I craved a reminder of His constant compassion; and through their obedience to extend hospitality, it powerfully reflected God's character.

OUR SOULS ACHE FOR AN INVITATION,
TO BE INCLUDED AND WELCOMED.

As women, our souls ache for an invitation, to be included and welcomed. This coming together in community, whether large or small, is central to how God has designed us; and yet this core extension of ourselves has somehow been lost in modern society.

Over and over again, the theme of biblical hospitality is woven throughout the tapestry of Scripture. Beginning in the Old Testament, God tells us to both welcome and love the strangers. Giving of oneself through time, energy, and meager possessions was demonstrated to traveling strangers by feeding and housing them after an exhausting journey.

As we see hospitality unveiled in the New Testament, it's a distinctive mark of the early Christian church. The home was noted as a place to extend grace to others, and they took that challenge seriously. As I searched Scripture and commentaries on this topic, I wanted to throw down a few crumbs for you to follow. The trail it leads us down convicts me anew because anytime Scripture uses such strong verbiage as "command," it causes me to pay attention.

In Romans 12:13 Paul states, "Pursue hospitality." It's not a question. In fact, pursue is a verb that implies continuous action. In pursuing hospitality, we are continually moving toward something; and in this pursuit of hospitality, it's a command, not a choice.

When I broke down the word "hospitality" from the original Greek word, *philoxenia*, I found it's a combination of two concepts. *Philo* is one of several words for love. Then *xenos* means stranger. Love of strangers.

There is no grand blueprint for biblical hospitality apart from simply loving others.

When I'm tempted to confuse entertaining (with its myriad of party planning tips, color schemes, and tablescapes) and hospitality, I'm reminded that there is no grand blueprint for biblical hospitality apart from simply loving others.

"Above all, love each other deeply . . . Offer [Show] hospitality to one another without grumbling [complaining]. Each of you should use whatever gift you have received to serve others, as faithful stewards of God's grace in its various forms" (1 Pet. 4:8–10 NIV, author's translation in brackets).

Both Paul and Peter link hospitality's theme to Christ's declaration to love others. To show hospitality is to love others. It doesn't get more straightforward than that. Let's note that Peter doesn't stop at "Offer [show] hospitality." He adds, "Offer [show] hospitality without grumbling." It reminds me of when our kids were younger and I'd ask them to do something. Often they'd obey but trudge through the motions. I'd always remind them, "Do it with a happy heart, please." I can almost hear Peter reminding us of the same.

Grumbling in this day and age often means excuses. "I don't have extra money in the budget. My kids are too young, my house is a mess, and our schedule is crazy."

Recently, before friends were coming over, my son yelled down the stairs, "Mom, why do we have to invite people over? I really do not feel like cleaning my room." (Let's just forget the fact that he had a week to clean it.) This attitude robbed him of a real blessing to give of himself to others.

Other times, grumbling manifests itself from a place of deep hurt. We've extended hospitality, and it's been rejected. We've opened our homes and been betrayed. Scabs still fresh cover our heart, and it's too painful to rip those open once again to trust.

John Piper states, "Grace is the hospitality of God to welcome sinners not because of their goodness but because of his glory."[22]

The ultimate gift of hospitality stretched the chasm when Jesus died to welcome all. No longer foreigners or strangers, those who accept His salvation gift find a home through Him.

So when our heart wrestles and questions our ability to vulnerably extend ourself once more, remember how often Christ pursues us and never gives up. Be defined by an all-consuming desire to grow more in the measure of His love for us and share with others the evidence of our life transformed. Proclaim His glory.

People often confuse the next portion of this passage, "Each of you should use whatever gift you have received to serve others," and interpret that to mean, "I don't have the gift of hospitality."

My best friend used to joke, "I only have the spiritual gift of treats because all I'm ever asked to do is bring brownies." She struggled to find her spiritual gift and never felt good enough to be the host. Repeatedly, I reminded her of how much food ministers. Practicing biblical hospitality is as simple as sharing a brownie wrapped in tin foil with a handwritten note tucked inside to brighten someone's day.

Remember that this Scripture isn't a suggestion, but a command. Biblical hospitality is not a gift that some have and others don't. It's simply a call to love others well. Scripture isn't addressing entertaining or throwing a lavish party. There are certainly times for that, and some find it much easier than others; but practically speaking, loving others through hospitality is sharing of your heart through time, offering a listening ear to someone in need, or sometimes, it looks like a pan of brownies.

Why do we tend to make it so difficult?

Because we make it too much about us. Extending hospitality is about freely giving of ourselves. When our focus shifts from us to them, it removes any unnecessary expectations. We pursue hospitality knowing that Christ is enough. We are enough through Him.

The heart of the gospel is rooted in hospitality; and at the core, both the heart of the gospel and hospitality are simple. They both invite the weary, the messy, the brokenhearted, the questioning to come and find rest. They both welcome the stranger and offer a refuge for our souls.

Jesus gathered many around the table, broke bread, and used that time to share some of the most profound truths of the gospel.

The fullness of God's grace, poured out in our lives, allows us to be the conduit by which hospitality and the gospel intersect.

The fullness of God's grace, poured out in our lives, allows us to be the conduit by which hospitality and the gospel intersect, even in those difficult times. Honestly, it's an honor to say yes to something for which I'm so unqualified.

Three weeks had passed since lunch with our new "elevator" friends. After church we stopped in the gym to let the boys run and crawl all their energy out. A young couple entered right behind us with their little boy, and we found out it was their very first week visiting our church.

We chatted for a while, and without any preplanning or overthinking, without taking time to worry if our home was clean or if I had a meal ready to go, I extended an invitation to relative strangers.

"I know it's last minute and we just met, but would your family like to come over for lunch today?"

Because one thing our elevator friends modeled for us is that our homes are on loan. We are merely the stewards of them, and with their one invitation it created a ripple effect.

Recently, I ran into the friends we met in the gym some twenty years ago. They ended up taking us up on our offer, which led to friendship, sharing pregnancies and the birth of babies together, and then lots of tentative conversations including, "How on earth do we raise these blessings without an instruction guide?" So we formed a couples' small group and, of course, invited them.

While we were catching up, she introduced me to her friend. "Jen and Gregg were the first people we met here. They invited us over on the spot and welcomed us immediately. We've never forgotten that."

The ripple effect. One invitation.

I told part of this story to a friend, and I immediately became choked up. The unexpected emotion I felt overwhelmed me because I'd lost touch with just how much impact a simple extension of Christ's love has on others. Rarely do we see the outcome, but in this case I did.

Tears streamed down my face, not shed from nice sentiments, but tears borne out of a gut-wrenching conviction asking how many other simple invitations did I miss extending?

My heart has been newly awakened to rediscover the New Testament teaching on hospitality.

Actively pursuing it throughout my day-to-day makes ordinary interactions purposeful.

I once heard, "The smallest acts of kindness are worth more than the grandest intention."

Life is full of grand intentions without follow-through. Christ followed through until His final breath; yet too often, I'm merely the "Queen of those Best Intentions" due to my own priorities. If we are commanded to show hospitality and love others as Christ loved the church, then may I practically demonstrate hospitality as a symbol of His work in my life. It's not always pretty. In fact, it's often quite messy, but I invite you to join me on this journey of imperfectly loving others together. I'd consider it such an honor.

CONNECTION QUESTIONS

1. How can we embrace the joy of practicing hospitality without viewing it as just one more obligation?

2. How can we use our homes to intentionally draw others into experiencing Christ's love?

3. Who are the "strangers" in your life that you can reach out to this week?

CONNECTION CHALLENGE

As you spend time with God today, ask Him to show you what hospitality looks like in your life. Not the version you find online or in someone else's home, but the kind of warm welcome He wants you to extend to someone who may simply need a friend today. Be the friend you wish you had and swing those doors wide open.

Gather your family or friends together and challenge everyone to be on the lookout for the first "new" person they meet. Invite them over. Is it a new coworker? Is it a child's classmate or the new neighbor down the street? Could it be a new family from church or a few college students? Let them know that there is always room at the table for them.

PRAYER

Lord, thank you for continually opening my eyes. I've been so convicted of my own self-centeredness when it comes to practicing biblical hospitality and determining when and where on my own terms. Often, I make it into something that it's not, and you've gently reminded me that you only ask me to simply love on others.

Oh Lord, I'm reminded that heartfelt hospitality listens. It welcomes. It looks for authentic conversations. Please open my eyes to intentionally look for opportunities to draw others in. Let my hospitality be the open canvas that allows the sharing and giving in community to become our tangible art. Amen.

Conclusion

As you close this book, we hope that you've wrecked it a little bit. Highlighted lines and folded-down pages, and notes written in margins—those are a few of our favorite things!

These words are our invitation to you—to the world-changers, visionaries, creators, dreamers, writers, life-embracers, encouragement-seekers. To the mamas, the sisters, the introverts, and extroverts. Wherever you are, whatever your passion, wherever you most need community—we want to invite you to join us to continue pursuing those connections you crave.

As these stories have been collected and we've journeyed together, we haven't just thought of you in passing or considered you a number or a book sale or a reader.

We have prayed for you.

We have had you on our hearts.

We have done more than make room among our stories—we have planned for you. There is a seat here, a space with your name on it, saved for you. Whether you join us on our website or gather friends to work through these challenges again as a book club, we hope you feel welcome to join us again.

If you've been searching for community, we are here, coming together off websites and social media. Among these pages and in our stories, we hope you've found a group of like-hearted sisters who came alongside you and said, "Me, too."

"You can develop a healthy, robust community that lives right with God and enjoy its results *only* if you do the hard work of getting along with each other, treating each other with dignity and honor" (James 3:18 MSG).

Finding community takes work. Choosing to stay in community takes even harder work. Being brave enough to share your story is nearly a superpower. But we have prayerfully gone first on these pages so that you can find courage in Christ to go next. And you've so bravely joined us on your own. Now, as we think about what's next:

- May you seek to connect with God more deeply as you pour over His Word.
- May you discover new ways to connect with friends more purposefully as you invite women into your story.
- May you connect intentionally with your community from the overflow of the love and grace and talents God pours into your life.

We hope you come back to these pages often to be encouraged when connecting with God and friends, and when community feels hard. Bring friends to these pages and journey together. Know that anywhere you find the women of (in)courage, you will find a place to come as you are, kick off your shoes, and find friendship, prayer, grace, and a shared love for Christ.

We are far from perfect, but we pray you find God-gifted community **where the expectations of perfect are left at the front door and the only hope is that Christ would fill in where we fail.**

"Therefore encourage one another and build each other up as you are already doing" (1 Thess. 5:11).

Author Q&A

At (in)courage, we like to take a little time to get to know one another with some fun questions. It's another way we hope you can find yourself among friends—and maybe even have a "Me, too!" moment as you read their answers.

Are you more likely to text, call, or e-mail a friend?

- **Angela Nazworth:** Phone call is my favorite, but I'm also known for sending quick "I think you're awesome" and other such texts to friends as encouragement.
- **Carey Bailey:** As a life coach I talk on the phone every day for a living, but I am actually a phone-a-phobic and would choose texting over dialing any day!
- **Anna Rendell:** Text, text, text. To the chagrin of my thirteen-year-old self who lived for the phone, I'm a notorious call screener—I never answer!
- **Kristen Strong:** I want my answer to be call them, but in real life it's text :)
- **Amanda White:** Texting is the way to my introverted heart—quiet, simple, and there are fun emojis!

What one food would you take to the proverbial desert island?

- **Denise Hughes:** I suppose I should say kale, but to be honest, I'd rather have french fries.
- **Tonya Salomons:** Just one!? If I must choose it would be cheese. That's because I'm imagining my island with fruit. So many options with cheese.

- **Crystal Stine:** Oh that's easy—chocolate wacky cake. I'm sure I'll find something healthy on the rest of the island!
- **Karina Allen:** This is an unfair question. I live in the south, so I like ALL the food! But I can always eat Mexican! It's chips and salsa for the win!
- **Eryn Hall:** If I was headed to the proverbial desert island, I'm not leaving home without my chips and salsa. #musthave

What role would you play in a rock band?

- **Robin Dance:** Adele, just Adele. Unforgettable voice, unconventional style. Moxie. And those cat-eyes . . .
- **Jennifer Dukes Lee:** In a rock band, I'm the one with three-inch-high '80s bangs. Also, I am kind of an air guitar legend. #HereIam #RockYouLikeAHurricane #AquaNet
- **Aliza Latta:** I would definitely be the drummer. Not that I could keep an actual beat, but I could whip my hair back and forth like there ain't no tomorrow.
- **Christine Wright:** Singer. Revival would surely be sparked (from all the people on their knees in prayer to stop the searing pain). #whateverittakes
- **Mary Carver:** Lead singer! Because singing harmony is hard, and I'm not coordinated enough to play the drums. And, FINE, because I'd like all the attention!

What do you find that you usually have in common with your friends?

- **Bonnie Gray:** I'm drawn to friends who speak from the soul, enjoy books and conversations over coffee, sharing stories, pastries, and quiet walks among the trees.
- **Holley Gerth:** My friends and I usually share a love for coffee, yoga pants, and Jesus (not in that order)!

- **Jennifer Ueckert:** I share a creativity connection with friends. It's the way we find best to communicate from the heart and what we understand in one another.
- **Stephanie Bryant:** I don't have a lot in common with my friends. There's a wide variety of personalities that make up my girl friends.
- **Erin Mohring:** My friends and I connect through several things, but we mostly have in common a love for Jesus, running, and our kids!

What makes you feel brave?

- **Kris Camealy:** When a friend invites me to be honest about my struggles, withholds their judgment, and reminds me of God's grace, I feel brave.
- **Annie Downs:** Listening to the dreams of my friends makes me feel brave. When they are brave, I feel like I can be too.
- **Jen Schmidt:** I always choose to have my family beside me. They make me feel brave.
- **Deidra Riggs:** God's proven track record in my life, over fifty-two years.
- **Dawn Camp:** When I feel like I'm stepping out in line with God's will: "If God be for us, who can be against us?" That makes me brave.

If you could have coffee with one fictional character, who would it be?

- **Kate Motaung:** I'd love to have tea with Jo from *Little Women* because of her spunk, her love for writing, and to ask why on earth she didn't marry Laurie.
- **Stacey Thacker:** Sydney Bristow. A little secret agent shoptalk shared over a latte and a muffin would come in handy in my everyday life as wife, mom, and writer.
- **Renee Swope:** Crosby from *Parenthood*

- **Lisa-Jo Baker:** Father Tim from the Mitford books, because he reminds me that changing the world can look like investing deeply in your friends.
- **Crystal Stine:** Doctor Who, because we could have coffee anywhere in the world, at any point in time.

Now it's your turn! Pick one of the questions above and share your answer on Facebook, Twitter, or Instagram. Tag @incourage and use the hashtag #cravingconnection—we can't wait to hear your thoughts!

Author Bios

At (in)courage our heart is for you to always find yourself in these stories shared by women in all ages and stages of life, living in different areas of the world, who all love Jesus. The friends who shared their stories on these pages represent the unique voices and experiences we celebrate at (in)courage. Married, single, working full-time in or out of the home, stay-at-home moms, empty nesters, young adults, city dwellers and rural farm girls and everything in between—we hope you've found yourself among friends. Here's a little more about each of the authors featured in *Craving Connection*:

Karina Allen: Karina is devoted to helping women live out their unique calling and building authentic community through practical application of Scripture in an approachable, winsome manner. You can connect with Karina at her blog, forhisnameandhisrenown. wordpress.com, monthly at incourage.me and purposefulfaith.com or @karina268 on Twitter.

Carey Bailey: Carey supports women in satisfying their cravings for abundant life through life coaching and teaching. You can connect with her at careybailey.com and withjoyretreats.com or @careycbailey on Instragram. She is the author of *Cravings: Desiring God in the Midst of Motherhood*, the co-owner of With Joy Retreats, and the creative director for Allume.

Lisa-Jo Baker: Lisa-Jo sincerely believes motherhood is a superpower and that the shortest distance between strangers and friends is a shared story. You can connect with Lisa-Jo at her blog, lisajo-baker.com, monthly at incourage.me, or @lisajobaker on Instagram.

She is the author of *Surprised by Motherhood: Everything I Never Expected About Being a Mom,* and she is the community manager for (in)courage.

Stephanie Bryant: Stephanie Bryant, cofounder of (in)courage, is enthusiastic about encouraging women to follow hard after God, listen to His voice, and be brave enough to do His will. Stephanie is thrilled for her own Jesus-led adventure with her husband, Barry, her daughter, Gabrielle, and Hank, the farm dog on their newly developed farm. You can follow along with Stephanie at www.BryantFamily.Farm and on instagram @StephanieSBryant as she learns the rhythm of grace in her new Promised Land.

Kris Camealy: Kris is passionate about bringing people to the table to be nourished by good words, good food, and Jesus. Meet Kris at her blog, kriscamealy.com and on Instagram @kriscamealy. Kris is the author of the book, *Holey, Wholly, Holy: A Lenten Journey of Refinement,* and the founder of GraceTable.org, a community Table open to all who are hungry for more of Jesus.

Dawn Camp: Dawn thrives at the intersection of family, faith, and Photoshop. You can connect with her at her blog, MyHomeSweetHomeOnline.net, monthly at incourage.me, @dawn-camp on Instagram, and @DawnMHSH on Twitter. Dawn is the editor and photographer of *The Beauty of Grace, The Gift of Friendship,* and *The Heart of Marriage.*

Mary Carver: Mary is a writer and speaker who shares stories from her imperfect life with humor and honesty, encouraging women to give up on perfect and get on with life. You can connect with Mary at her blog, givinguponperfect.com, monthly at incourage.me and MomAdvice.com, or @marycarver on Twitter. Mary is the coauthor of *Choose Joy: Finding Hope and Purpose When Life Hurts* and editorial assistant at ForEveryMom.com.

Robin Dance: Married to her college sweetheart and mama to three, Robin is growing more in love with people everyday—she really wants to know *your* story. Find her writing at robindance. me, monthly at incourage.me and theartofsimple.net, and as @ PensieveRobin on Instagram. She's collaborated on a few special book projects, and in the hopes of encouraging parents during a season many often dread, she wrote a series on parenting teens and tweens.

Annie F. Downs: Annie F. Downs is an author, blogger, and speaker based in Nashville, Tennessee. Flawed but funny, she uses her writing to highlight the everyday goodness of a real and present God. An author of four books—*Looking for Lovely*, *Let's All Be Brave*, *Perfectly Unique*, and *Speak Love*, Annie also loves traveling around the country speaking to young women, college students, and adults. Read more at anniefdowns.com and follow her on Twitter @ anniefdowns.

Holley Gerth: Holley Gerth loves encouraging women to embrace who they are, become all God created them to be, and live intentionally. She'd love to have coffee with you, and until then you can connect with her at www.holleygerth.com. Holley is the *Wall Street Journal* best-selling author of several books, including *You're Already Amazing*.

Bonnie Gray: Bonnie Gray brews words for your soul and rest for the journey of faith, serving up encouragement, soul care, and stories at incourage.me, *Relevant* magazine, and Crosswalk. You can connect with Bonnie on her blog, FaithBarista.com, or online @thebonniegray on Facebook and Instagram. Author of *Finding Spiritual Whitespace: Awakening Your Soul to Rest*, Bonnie is a speaker and host of her podcast *Coffee Break for Your Soul*—a conversation between friends to refresh your heart and inspire your story in everyday life.

Eryn Hall: Eryn has a heart for encouraging women to make the most of every day. She occasionally journals at MamaHall. com but more frequently shares snapshots of life @mamahall on Instagram. Eryn is one of the hostesses of Declare, a conference for women seeking to know God and make Him known.

Denise Hughes: As an English teacher, Denise loves the world of words, where life and literature connect, but she's most passionate about the one Book with living words—the Word of God. She's the author of two Bible studies, *Word Writers: Ephesians* and *Word Writers: Philippians*, and she's the founder of deeperwaters.us, a ministry devoted to spiritual formation where women can gather and grow deeper together. You can find Denise writing on her blog denisejhughes.com and at (in)courage, where she enjoys serving as the editorial coordinator.

Aliza Latta: Aliza Latta is a young Canadian writer, storyteller, artist, and hand letterer—and is a big believer in both courage and ice cream. You can connect with Aliza on her blog, www.alizanaomi.com, or as @alizalatta on Twitter and Instagram. You can also check out Aliza's online shop, Choose Brave, www.etsy.com/shop/choosebrave, where she shares her hand-lettered and water-colored artwork.

Jennifer Dukes Lee: Jennifer is a storyteller and a grace dweller who loves messy people and Jesus. You can connect with Jennifer at her blog, JenniferDukesLee.com, monthly at incourage. me, or @dukeslee on Instagram and Twitter. Jennifer is the author of *The Happiness Dare* and *Love Idol*.

Erin Mohring: Erin lives with her husband and their three sons in Nebraska, where she enjoys running, reading, and eating popcorn. You can connect with her on her personal blog, homewiththeboys.net, and on all social media at @homewiththeboys (Instagram is her favorite). She is the cofounder of Raising Boys Ministries and

The MOB Society, as well as a contributing writer for Tommy Nelson and *ParentLife* magazine.

Kate Motaung: Kate and her South African husband have three children, and they all live with hearts divided between West Michigan and South Africa. You can find Kate at her blog, katemotaung.com, or on Twitter at @k8motaung.

Angela Nazworth: Angela Nazworth is passionate about living life with a heart wide open. She writes mostly about the beauty of grace, friendship, vulnerability, and community for incourage.me and on her personal blog, angelanazworth.com.

Anna Rendell: Anna Rendell fits writing into the margins of her day and has a heart for offering real encouragement to real women. Author of *A Moment of Christmas: Daily Advent Devotions for Timestrapped Moms* and *Mom Prayers: 25 Everyday Prayers for Real Moms*, Anna is also the social media coordinator at (in)courage. Connect with Anna at her blog, girlwithblog.com, monthly at incourage.me, and @girlwithblog on Instagram and Facebook.

Deidra Riggs: Deidra is a national speaker and writer who works to build bridges and tear down the walls that divide us—in our culture, our neighborhoods, our hearts, and the Church. Engage the conversation with Deidra and her community at her website, DeidraRiggs.com, each month at incourage.me, or @deidrariggs on Instagram (her favorite) and Twitter, and follow on Facebook. Deidra is the author of *Every Little Thing: Making a World of Difference Right Where You Are.*

Jen Schmidt: As a mom of five, Jen is passionate about encouraging women to find beauty amidst the bedlam of everyday life. You can connect with her at beautyandbedlam.com, 10minutedinners.com, and Facebook @beautyandbedlam. Jen is the cohost of the annual Becoming Conference.

Tonya Salomons: Tonya falls in love with community every single day and believes that your story is the music that her story needs to hear. You can find her writing over at stonetoheart.com, and she is a regular contributor at gracetable.org where she writes about hospitality and coming to the table with Jesus. Tonya also loves being on Instagram and can be found at @stonetoheart. Currently, Tonya lives by the hashtag #studentmom as she is finishing her undergraduate degree at Western University in Southwestern, Ontario, Canada and will be completing her Master's degree in social work in the next year.

Crystal Stine: Crystal is passionate about cultivating a community where faith, fitness, and friendship come together. Married to her high-school sweetheart and mama to a little girl, you can connect with Crystal on her blog, crystalstine.me, or @crystalstine on Instagram and Twitter. Author of *Creative Basics: 30 Days to Awesome Social Media Art*, Crystal is an author, editor, speaker, event MC, coach, and serves as the host of write31days.com—a yearly writing challenge.

Kristen Strong: Kristen is wife to her retired Air Force veteran, mama to three priority blessings, and fresh-air giver who loves helping women see themselves as Jesus does. Kristen blogs regularly at chasingblueskies.net, once a month at incourage.me, and frequents her favorite social media tool Instagram. She is the author of *Girl Meets Change*, a book that helps women see their difficult life change in a more hopeful light.

Renee Swope: Renee Swope is a Word-lover, heart-encourager, storyteller, and grace-needer who loves to empower and equip women with courage and confidence to make a difference right where they are, with the unique gifts, passions, stories, and experiences they already have! She is a speaker, radio cohost, and best-selling author of *A Confident Heart* and *A Confident Heart Devotional*. Connect with Renee online at ReneeSwope.com, monthly at incourage.me, @reneeswope on Instagram and Twitter, or in her Facebook communities: facebook.com/aconfidentheart and facebook.com/reneeswope.

Stacey Thacker: Stacey is Mike's wife and the mother of four vibrant girls. You can connect with her at staceythacker.com or on Instagram @staceythacker where she loves to encourage women to grow in faith and talks about the really important stuff of life like cardigans and coffee. She is the coauthor of *Hope for the Weary Mom* and the author of *Fresh Out of Amazing*.

Jennifer Ueckert: Jennifer uses her passion for art to encourage, inspire, and remind people of His love. You can connect with Jennifer on her site, studiojru.com, where she continually has new original paintings, crosses, and art prints or @studiojru on Instagram.

Amanda White: Amanda likes to think up fun ways to tell her kids about Jesus and likes to share those ideas with others. Most of those ideas are on her blog, ohAmanda.com, and the new ones she's trying out usually show up on Instagram @oohamanda. Thousands of families have used and enjoyed her family devotional books, *Truth in the Tinsel: an Advent Experience for Little Hands* and *A Sense of the Resurrection: an Easter Experience for Families* to celebrate Jesus throughout the year.

Christine Wright: Christine is the least likely prayer warrior, whose knees knock when she's asked to pray out loud. She writes for GodsizedDreams.com and christianwomensvoice.org. Christine can also be found helping to facilitate monthly revivalprayerconnection. com gatherings.

Notes

1. C. S. Lewis, *A Grief Observed* (New York, NY: Seabury Press, 1961).

2. John Piper, http://www.desiringgod.org/messages/christs-power-is-made-perfect-in-weakness (July 14, 1991).

3. Gil Bailie, *Violence Unveiled* (Spring Valley, NY: Crossroad Publishing, 1996), xv.

4. John Ortberg, *Soul Keeping: Caring for the Most Important Part of You* (Grand Rapids, MI: Zondervan, 2014).

5. F. B. Meyer, Precept Austin.org, http://www.preceptaustin.org/how_to_handle_fear_%281%29.htm, accessed January 18, 2016.

6. Amy Carmichael, *Towards Jerusalem*, "The Age-Long Minute" (Washington, PA: CLC 2013).

7. Matthew Henry, *Matthew Henry's Commentary on the Bible*, accessed January 19, 2016, www.biblestudytools.com/commentaries/matthew-henry-complete/isaiah/41.html.

8. Strong's Concordance, *Bible Hub*, s.v. "forgive," accessed January 31, 2016, http://Biblehub.com/greek/859.htm.

9. Merriam-Webster, *Merriam-Webster's Collegiate Dictionary* (Springfield, MA: Merriam-Webster, Inc., 2003).

10. Philip Yancey, *What's So Amazing About Grace?* (Grand Rapids, MI: Zondervan, 1997), 123.

11. Corrie ten Boom, *I Stand at the Door and Knock: Meditations by the Author of The Hiding Place* (Grand Rapids, MI: Zondervan, 2008), 62). Kindle Edition.

12. "3 Reasons to Stop Comparing Yourselves to Others," *Psychology Today*, accessed at https://www.psychologytoday.com/

blog/bouncing-back/201508/3-reasons-stop-comparing-yourself-others.

13. Mary C. Lamia, PhD, "Jealousy and Envy: The Emotions of Comparison and Contrast," *Psychology Today* (July 13, 2013). Accessed at https://www.psychologytoday.com/blog/intense-emotions-and-strong-feelings/201307/jealousy-and-envy-the-emotions-comparison-and.

14. Brené Brown, *Daring Greatly: How the Courage to be Vulnerable Transforms the Way We Live, Parent, and Lead* (New York, NY: Gotham Books, 2012).

15. See http://biblehub.com/commentaries/cambridge/ecclesiastes/4.htm.

16. See http://www.livescience.com/16879-close-friends-decrease-today.html.

17. See https://www.thebowencenter.org/theory/eight-concepts/triangles.

18. See http://www.incourage.me/2010/09/roped-together.html.

19. See https://www.goodreads.com/quotes/18064-kind-words-can-be-short-and-easy-to-speak-but.

20. See http://www.inc.com/peter-economy/26-brilliant-quotes-on-the-super-power-of-words.html.

21. See http://www.biblestudytools.com/commentaries/matthew-henry-concise/romans/12.html.

22. John Piper, "Strategic Hospitality," August 25, 1985, http://www.desiringgod.org/messages/strategic-hospitality.

craving connection | (in)courage

Download
your *free printables* today!

Resources and tools to help you
connect with God, friends, & community.

Visit **www.incourage.me/cravingconnection**
to download your free printables.

Check list, coloring pages, invitation, notes, recipe cards, & more!

(in)courage

Gifts, Stationery & Cards

Listening to the Lord
and our community
helps us create products
that equip you to make
meaningful connections
with other women.

Available in retail stores
&
dayspring.com

Helping women find a place of

faith, connection & friendship

At (in)courage you are always welcome,
just the way you are.
You're surrounded by grace,
loved unconditionally and never alone.

Whether you're single or have great-grandkids.
Whether you're a mama, an artist, an
entrepreneur, or a book lover. Whether you
stay at home or work full time. Whether you're
outgoing or prefer an afternoon alone.
Come share. Come connect.

You'll always find yourself among friends.

Follow us on Social Media!
@incourage

www.incourage.me